Rebuilding a Bipartisan Consensus on Trade Policy

Phil Levy
Senior Fellow, Global Economy
Chicago Council on Global Affairs

April 2019

Contents

Boxes

Figures

Table

Chapter I: Introduction

We're in a mess now

By the summer of 2018, the United States was ramping up its first real trade war since the 1930s. The Trump administration was slapping tariffs on Chinese imports and responding to Chinese retaliation with escalation. The closest US allies were hit with tariffs on steel and aluminum on the grounds that trade in these products posed a national security threat. The Trump administration was detailing the flaws of the World Trade Organization (WTO) and using its power to block new appointments to the WTO's dispute settlement system. The Trans-Pacific Partnership (TPP) trade deal that the United States had spearheaded was proceeding without US participation. The system of rules-based trade that had been built largely to US specifications was rapidly being dismantled, and American farmers and businesses were starting to feel the effects.

How did it come to this? How did trade become a central issue of the 2016 presidential election? Why was the country turning back to the sort of protectionism that had been discredited during the Great Depression?

More importantly, how can the country navigate its way out of this mess? What options are there for new and different approaches? And what happens if those fail?

As prelude, we can set the scene for the turning-point 2016 election. We go back to the early 1990s, when a rift developed between Republicans and Democrats over trade. Neither party was pure in its opposition or support of agreements, but Republicans tilted toward supporting deals and Democrats tilted against.

In the 1992 presidential election, George H. W. Bush was running as the incumbent against Bill Clinton. Bush had overseen the negotiation of the North American Free Trade Agreement (NAFTA). Clinton had assumed leadership of a party that was skeptical of the deal. When Clinton won, he had to decide what to do with the agreement, which had been signed but not approved by Congress. He ultimately declared NAFTA would be acceptable if it were accompanied by new side agreements covering labor and environmental issues.

This maneuver sufficed to get NAFTA passed in 1993, but it also shaped the partisan rift for decades to come. Democrats in Congress were wary of trade deals and pushed for subsequent agreements to include strong language on labor and the environment. Republicans in Congress were generally more enthused but wary of labor or environmental measures that might push rules beyond existing domestic law. Despite the apparent partisan split, presidents from both parties pushed for the negotiation and passage of trade deals, whatever stance they might have taken on the campaign trail.

The ensuing deals, and there were many, sometimes faced years of delay but ultimately squeaked through Congress. The supporting majorities were heavily, though not exclusively, Republican. For those who opposed the trade deals, the issue remained an effective—and politically potent—rallying cry.

At the presidential level, Democratic candidates would express skepticism about trade deals and gather support from groups who disliked them, in particular organized labor. Republican candidates would express more enthusiasm and draw support from business and agricultural communities that favored the liberalization the deals brought.

Upon taking office, each new president would ultimately embrace trade deals, either as the fulfillment of a longtime stance (George W. Bush) or because their analysis of economic and foreign policy imperatives led them there (Bill Clinton and Barack Obama). For the Democrats, the conversion generally required some face-saving change to existing agreements. Clinton had the NAFTA side letters. Obama oversaw minor renegotiations of pending deals.[1]

In 2016 things seemed to be proceeding according to pattern. The incumbent president, Obama, had a negotiated, but unpassed, deal (TPP). If there was to be sufficient support in Congress to pass TPP, it was going to come primarily from Republicans, as congressional Democrats were largely opposed. During that year's presidential campaign, Hillary Clinton, the Democratic candidate, declared her opposition to the deal, even though she had helped craft it as Secretary of State in Obama's first term. Nevertheless, this was still following the playbook—Democratic candidates express skepticism on the presidential campaign trail.

---

1. Since these renegotiations were sufficiently minor, the United States International Trade Commission, which evaluates trade deals, did not even perform new analyses on the revised agreements.

To complete the pattern, all that was required was a Republican candidate who embraced trade deals. There were plenty who might have filled the role. While most of the major establishment candidates in the Republican primaries refrained from explicitly endorsing TPP, Senators Ted Cruz and Marco Rubio and Governors Jeb Bush and John Kasich all seemed poised to adopt the traditional pro-trade role that awaited them.

The likely outcome seemed clear: TPP would either pass in the lame-duck period after the election, or the new president would make some tweaks and push the deal through. The perilous but predictable path for setting global trade rules would continue.

Then the pattern broke. Donald Trump captured the Republican nomination. He was vigorously skeptical of NAFTA, of TPP, and of trade deals in general. Hillary Clinton, who had anticipated an attack from the right on trade issues, instead faced a strong attack from the left. Neither her inclination nor her expertise positioned her well to outdo Trump in antipathy toward trade deals.

Trade ended up playing the most salient role in a US presidential election it had played since at least the 1992 campaign. While one can never say a US presidential campaign revolves entirely around a single issue, trade featured prominently in speeches and debates and seemed especially critical in the battle for key industrial states such as Michigan, Ohio, Pennsylvania, and Wisconsin. All of those states flipped from Democratic in 2012 to Republican in 2016.

Glimmers of hope

Given that both major party presidential candidates opposed TPP in the 2016 election and the tenuous congressional margins for recent trade deals—particularly in the House of Representatives—it might be tempting to conclude that the American people have turned against international trade and trade deals. However, there is ample evidence to the contrary.

In the summer of 2015, when TPP negotiations had yet to conclude, the Chicago Council on Global Affairs asked survey respondents, "As you may know, the United States is now negotiating a free trade agreement with twelve Pacific nations called the Trans-Pacific Partnership (or TPP). Based on what you know, do you strongly support, somewhat support, somewhat oppose, or strongly oppose this free trade agreement?"[2]

Note how stacked this question was against support. Even a strong trade advocate might have hesitated to support the agreement, sight unseen. Yet 64 percent of respondents indicated some or strong support and only 29 percent opposed. Before the vilification of the agreement in the 2016 campaign, there was strikingly strong public support.

The survey results yielded another surprise. A big trade vote in the House of Representatives in June 2015[3] had shown heavy support for trade deals among Republicans (191 in favor, 54 opposed) and serious doubts among Democrats (28 in favor, 157 opposed). But when the survey took into account respondents' self-identified party affiliation, Democrats came out on top, backing TPP 72 to 23 percent, compared to Republican support of 60 to 32 percent.

One might have thought that the denunciations of 2016 would have taken a toll on support for trade. To some extent, they did. Yet public support remained strong throughout and rose in 2017. In both 2016 and 2017, the Chicago Council Survey asked, "Overall, do you think international trade is good or bad for the US economy?"[4] The percentage of favorable responses rose from 59 percent in 2016 to 72 percent in 2017.

Of course, there is an important distinction between *trade* and *trade agreements*. After all, a core Trump contention in the 2016 campaign was that the United States had struck terrible trade deals—and that he could strike better ones. One interpretation was that trade itself was not so bad so long as one did not flub the rules.

Yet in the summer of 2017, on the eve of NAFTA renegotiation, 53 percent of survey respondents thought NAFTA was good for the US economy. Further, 57 percent of respondents thought trade deals either mostly benefited the United States or benefited *both* the United States and its partners. In both questions, a partisan split had developed in which a majority of Democrats held a favorable view of deals while only a minority of Republicans did.

---

2. Phil Levy, "The TPP Train Could Still Get Derailed," *Foreign Policy*, January 6, 2016, https://foreignpolicy.com/2016/01/06/pp-could-still-get-derailed-us-congress.

3. This was the vote for Trade Promotion Authority.

4. Dina Smeltz and Karen Whisler, *Pro-Trade Views on the Rise, Partisan Divisions on NAFTA Widen* (Chicago: The Chicago Council on Global Affairs, August 14, 2017), https://www.thechicagocouncil.org/publication/pro-trade-views-rise-partisan-divisions-nafta-widen.

One way to explain the discrepancy between public support and congressional votes could be the important role of interest groups. Republicans have traditionally drawn support from the business and agricultural communities, while Democrats have often relied on organized labor. Even though these divisions are not hard and fast, it would be challenging for Republicans to take a stance opposed by the US Chamber of Commerce, just as it would be tough for Democrats to back a proposal opposed by the AFL-CIO. Both organizations can provide critical support to candidates in terms of money and organization come election time. In recent decades, the business community has backed free trade agreements (FTAs), while organized labor has opposed them. Given that, it is not too difficult to see how the positions of members of Congress could drift from those of their constituents.

Nevertheless, the relatively positive polling for trade deals offers a degree of hope, particularly as it comes in the face of relentless criticism and protectionist acts. Prior to 2016 there had been relatively few voices offering stout defenses of trade. From a candidate's perspective, the embrace of a trade agreement had at least two clear disadvantages. It might mean telling a middle-aged former factory worker that the solutions to his problems were not so simple as revoking NAFTA. Or it might mean embracing every contentious element of sprawling agreements—and being held publicly responsible for them.

Business and agriculture often knew the value of the agreements, but usually only rallied when a pro-trade candidate was going to take a stand (rare of late) or when a big trade vote was coming. Because the Obama administration never put TPP before Congress for a vote, the last such public fight for a deal was in 2011.

We know, however, how much the commercial sector cares. It was clear when President Trump attempted to withdraw from NAFTA in April 2017. The reaction, as described by one prominent business lobbyist, was a "five-alarm fire." The outcry from business and agriculture seemed to play a critical role in stopping the withdrawal and prompting Trump to open talks on NAFTA renegotiation. This threat, coupled with mounting barriers to trade in 2018, brought trade into the public eye. The discussion shined a light on those who had benefited from open trade, not just those who claimed to have lost. By the summer of 2018, public support for trade hit the highest levels measured in the Chicago Council Survey.[5]

Too many disconnects

The purpose of this monograph is to offer a primer on the rapidly shifting trade situation. Chapter 2 begins by retracing the country's steps—how did we get to our present position, starting from the shattered global economic system following World War II? It goes on to consider two of the most salient issues in the trade debate: the fate of the US manufacturing sector and the role of China in the global trading system. Chapter 3 delves into some of the particular issues that have been the most contentious, from trade's alleged role in destroying manufacturing jobs, to dispute settlement, to trade deficits. Chapter 4 then explores paths the country might take to try moving toward a nonpartisan consensus on trade. These range from changes in how we negotiate trade agreements, to changes in how we perceive and describe trade agreements, to changes in the institutions supporting trade agreements.

The monograph's goal is to respectfully represent the different sides of the vigorous debate. This does not mean that all arguments will be accepted as valid. Some prominent ones are demonstrably wrong. But the work does strive to give each side an honest hearing.

The concluding chapter will address the importance of finding a path back to a trade policy that is less riven by partisan strife. That includes highlighting the dire consequences of failure and an embrace of isolation as well as the potential rewards that await a United States that conquers its qualms about global engagement and is able to reclaim its traditional leadership position.

---

5.   Dina Smeltz et al., *America Engaged: American Public Opinion and US Foreign Policy* (Chicago: The Chicago Council on Global Affairs, 2018), https://digital.thechicagocouncil.org/america-engaged?_ga=2.258877839.482070157.1547582270-1518113569.1485877455.

Chapter II: How did we get to this point?

There are at least three reasons why a discussion of the way forward on trade policy should begin with a look backward. The first is that there are lessons to be learned from experience, as with the cautionary tales of past trade wars. The second is that some central points in current debates are essentially historical. Were past trade agreements unfair? Why did countries not drop tariffs reciprocally on goods like autos? The third is that understanding what has come before can be a useful way to begin studying topics and issues that would otherwise seem dauntingly complex.

This chapter is broken into three parts. The first offers a quick account of some major historical issues and landmarks in trade, dating back to 1930.[6] The second delves into the issue of manufacturing, which has been a particularly salient issue in recent debates. The third discusses the history of China in the global trading system.

History of the postwar trading system

Reacting to the breakdown: Smoot-Hawley

In recent political discussions, it is sometimes implied that the United States pursued the open, postwar trading order out of a blind, ideological commitment to free trade and that it willfully neglected the impacts on workers and industries damaged by competition. A novel and smarter policy, the implication goes, might be to judiciously apply tariffs and quotas to protect US industry.

Consider the following quote:

> Certain provisions of the present law require revision in the light of changes in the world competitive situation. . . . We realize that there are certain industries which cannot now successfully com-

---

6.   For a magisterial and thorough treatment of the history of US trade policy, see Douglas A. Irwin, *Clashing over Commerce: A History of US Trade Policy* (Chicago: The University of Chicago Press, 2017), on which this section draws.

pete with foreign producers because of lower foreign wages and a lower cost of living abroad, and we pledge the next Republican Congress to an examination and, where necessary, a revision of these schedules to the end that American labor in these industries may again command the home market, may maintain its standard of living, and may count upon steady employment in its accustomed field.[7]

There are two giveaways that this is not a modern proclamation of how to "Make America Great Again." First, there is the slightly archaic language. Second, there is the reference to the Republican Congress (as opposed to the president) as the driving force in boosting protection. Otherwise, the ideas could have come from 2016.

In fact, this was the Republican Party platform of 1928. Republicans went on to win the election, controlling the House, the Senate, and the presidency (Herbert Hoover). They followed through on their platform pledge and passed the Smoot-Hawley Tariff Act of 1930.[8]

Furthering the historical parallels, economists at the time warned of the damage the package might do. They were dismissed on the grounds that they "have not the slightest practical knowledge."[9] The vast majority of newspaper editorial pages—238 out of 324—argued against the policy, but to no avail.[10] The push for protection began at a time when the economy was relatively strong, and unemployment was fairly low.[11]

So what did the Smoot-Hawley Tariff Act do? It raised tariffs on 890 items, lowered them on 235, and left 2,170 unchanged.[12] On average, the tariff rose to 41.14 percent from 35.65 percent, an increase of

---

7.   Donald B. Johnson and Kirk H. Porter, *National Party Platforms, 1840-1972*, 5th ed. (Urbana: University of Illinois Press, 1973), 282, quoted in Irwin, *Clashing over Commerce*, 372–73.

8.   Technically, this should be the Hawley-Smoot Act, as it originated in the House, where Rep. Willis Hawley chaired the Ways and Means Committee. However, Sen. Reed Smoot has somehow received first billing in popular parlance, so we stick with that convention here.

9.   Cong. Rec. 1368 (daily ed. January 10, 1930) (statement of Sen. Reed Smoot), quoted in Irwin, *Clashing over Commerce*, 383.

10.   Irwin, *Clashing over Commerce*, 386.

11.   That changed, of course, with the onset of the Great Depression. But those economic events came after the Smoot-Hawley Tariff Act was well advanced toward passage.

12.   Irwin, *Clashing over Commerce*, 389.

5.5 percentage points—though with the number of unchanged and decreased items, that reflected greater changes in the goods for which tariffs rose. For comparison, in 2016 the average weighted tariff rate in the United States was 1.67 percent.[13]

By the fall of 1932, US imports had fallen 41 percent from mid-1930. Most of this was due to the sharp drop in real gross domestic product (GDP). The Smoot-Hawley tariffs may have accounted for about half of that drop, with the rest due to the contraction of real GDP.[14]

What part did the tariffs play in the Great Depression and the breakdown of the global economic system that followed? To quote Douglas A. Irwin:

> Because the Depression followed so closely on the heels of the tariff increase, many people at the time believed that the Hawley-Smoot tariff was responsible for the economic disaster. However . . . the consensus among economic historians is that monetary and financial factors were the dominant cause of the Great Depression. . . . While it was not responsible for the Great Depression, the Hawley-Smoot tariff contributed to the severe deterioration in trade relations in the early 1930s.[15]

But it was not only that the United States instituted these tariffs. Once the United States applied tariffs, other countries did the same under the similar guise of protecting domestic industries. The combined effect of countries turning inward aggravated the global slowdown.

The episode is important both as a failed experiment in redirecting demand toward domestic suppliers and as the inspiration for many of the institutions and policies that followed and shaped US policy and the global trading system to the present day.

---

13.   The World Bank, "Tariff Rate, Applied, Weighted Mean, All Products (%)" (data on the United States, Washington, DC: The World Bank), https://data .worldbank.org/indicator/TM.TAX.MRCH.WM.AR.ZS?locations=US.

14.   Irwin, *Clashing over Commerce*, 395–96. The tariffs may have had significantly more impact than intended because they were often *specific* (e.g., 5¢/bushel) rather than *ad valorem* (e.g., 5%). That meant that when deflation struck, the tariffs ended up representing a higher percentage of the value.

15.   Irwin, *Clashing over Commerce*, 397, 400.

Fast-track/trade promotion authority

A first such inspiration involved the way the United States negotiates trade deals. Article 1, Section 8 of the US Constitution grants the authority to Congress "to regulate Commerce with foreign Nations."[16]

Yet two serious problems developed with congressional control of the trade process. The first stemmed from the Smoot-Hawley experience. That tariff-setting process took place almost exclusively in Congress, as President Hoover remained mostly out of the debate. As the bill worked its way through the House and the Senate, there was sharp criticism of a process in which the levels of protection escalated through the practice of "log rolling," such as when a congressman from a sugar-producing district might agree to support protection for oranges in exchange for a sugar-protection vote from a colleague in an orange-producing district. The process was seen as promoting parochial interests at the expense of the national interest. It was presumed that any US president would be less likely to be a protectionist than Congress and more likely to take broader national interests into account.

The second problem concerned negotiation. While the Congresses that passed the tariff acts of 1922 and 1930 viewed the moves as largely domestic policy, the reaction to Smoot-Hawley made it clear that other countries would object to protection and that their retaliatory actions could damage the US economy. Once one recognized the potential gains from coordinating policies across countries, the importance of negotiation became clear. But having the United States represented by members of the House and the Senate posed practical difficulties.

To deal with these issues, Congress passed the Reciprocal Trade Agreements Act of 1934.[17] That delegated authority to the president to negotiate reciprocal trade deals with other countries, according to specifications set by Congress. It was the first of a series of such measures that largely took detailed tariff setting out of Congress' hands and assigned the task to the president. Subsequent measures were known as "fast-track," or currently, trade promotion authority (TPA).

---

16. U.S. Const. art. I, § 8, https://www.usconstitution.net/xconst_A1Sec8.html.
17. J. F. Hornbeck and William H. Cooper, *Trade Promotion Authority and the Role of Congress in Trade Policy* (Washington, DC: Congressional Research Service, April 7, 2011), http://www.au.af.mil/au/awc/awcgate/crs/rl33743.pdf.

The defining characteristics of the modern versions are:
1. The authority is granted for a limited time.
2. Legislation instructs the executive branch on negotiating objectives and sets reporting and consultation requirements.
3. The legislation eases the path of any resulting agreement through Congress.
4. The measures retain for Congress the ultimate right to vote for or against an agreement.

The reporting and consultation requirements are important in that they set the tempo of modern US trade negotiations. Frequently, there have been pushes to conclude trade agreements before the authority expires. The reporting and consultation limits constrain how quickly a president can act on trade deals.

The easing of the path has several key components. TPA sets rules whereby neither the House nor the Senate can amend a trade deal before it is signed, as amendments could undo a negotiated deal. It does not allow a filibuster in the Senate, so simple majorities suffice. It also places limits on how long Congress may take to consider a deal, though the time limits are quite long.[18]

This negotiating authority has often defined the terrain on which US trade policy battles are fought. In the late 1990s, Clinton could not get new negotiation authority because of arguments in Congress about the appropriate role of labor and environmental regulation in trade deals. Bush narrowly won TPA in 2002, but it expired in 2007. Obama did not win TPA until a very contentious battle in 2015, which meant that he was unable to advance his key trade measures until it was too late. Trump encountered TPA when he entered office and demanded a renegotiation of NAFTA. He found that he could not even begin negotiations until 90 days after his trade negotiators had notified Congress, per TPA requirements. He also found that he ran out of time to conclude the negotiations in the summer of 2018 because of TPA-mandated actions that had to occur between the end of negotiations and a congressional vote.

While TPA and its predecessors seem to cede authority over trade policy from the legislative branch to the executive, it is really just a loan.

---

18. The time limits for Congress total a maximum of 90 legislative days—days when the relevant chamber is in session. As Congress meets intermittently, this time period can last well over half a year.

It is a means whereby Congress retains its constitutional authority, but the administration conducts negotiations. Given the potential for a split between the White House and Congress, most trading partners are reluctant to trust the United States in negotiations until such a review process is in place. Not only are there formal requirements for the White House to consult with Congress during negotiations, the ultimate requirement that Congress vote up or down on a deal means that administrations must pay careful attention to congressional sentiment on trade if they want to be successful.

GATT world

Much of the institution-building of the post-World War II era was intended to remedy the breakdowns of the 1930s. The disruption of international financial relations inspired the creation of the International Monetary Fund. The failed, indebted states of the interwar period helped inspire the International Bank for Reconstruction and Development (a.k.a., the World Bank).

There was supposed to be a third such institution—the International Trade Organization (ITO)—but the United States ultimately did not agree to the negotiated terms and the ITO died.[19]

While the ITO was under negotiation, two dozen countries negotiated a provisional measure known as the General Agreement on Tariffs and Trade (GATT), with the first agreement struck in 1947.[20] This provisional arrangement ended up lasting until the creation of the WTO in 1994.

The GATT did not begin with an oath of fealty to free trade. It had some basic articles that described good behavior, but it was best thought of as a bargaining bazaar where countries would gather to strike mutually beneficial commercial deals. Deals would be struck through negotiating "rounds," in which countries would gather to make requests and offers. The requests would generally be for other countries to lower their trade barriers. The offers showed the willingness of a country to lower its own barriers.

---

19.   "From the GATT to the WTO: A Brief Overview" (research guide, Washington, DC: Georgetown Law Library), last modified September 25, 2018, http://guides.ll.georgetown.edu/c.php?g=363556&p=4108235.

20.   "The GATT Years: From Havana to Marrakesh," World Trade Organization, https://www.wto.org/english/thewto_e/Whatis_e/tif_e/fact4_e.htm.

Trump has criticized these deals on the grounds that they were not *reciprocal*.[21] In fact, they were, just not quite in the way he meant. The GATT rules required only that, for any given good, a participating country maintain the same tariff levels against all GATT countries. Thus, Japan *could not* have a 20 percent tariff on US autos but a 15 percent tariff on Canadian autos. This would have been a violation of most-favored nation (MFN) treatment.[22] The effect of the MFN rule was that an importing country would face the same tariffs on imports from all its GATT partners and would then, presumably, buy from whichever country could produce the good most efficiently.

Beyond the MFN restriction, countries could offer whatever package of tariff cuts they wanted. The United States might offer to cut its auto tariffs in half if Japan were to cut its tariffs on machine tools by two-thirds. This gets at the difference between *symmetry* and *reciprocity*. A country did not need to mirror the actions taken by another country. It *did* need to offer a package of cuts that was deemed to be of similar value.

Different countries, of course, could place very different values on the same tariff cut. If the United States was more interested in exporting machine tools than autos to Japan, it might value machine tool tariff cuts more highly. Further, there is no reason why a 50 percent cut in tariffs in one sector would have the same economic effect as a 50 percent cut in tariffs in another sector. The balance would depend on economic factors such as the shape of demand and supply curves and political factors such as the perceived importance of the industry.

The upshot is that GATT rounds were reciprocal. Countries felt they were adequately compensated for any concessions they made. They had to feel that way since the GATT operated on *consensus* rather than on majority rule. In theory, any aggrieved country could bring negotiations to a halt. However, the GATT approach to reciprocity did *not* guar-

---

21.   "What Donald Trump Means by Fair Trade," *The Economist*, May 13, 2017, https://www.economist.com/briefing/2017/05/13/what-donald-trump-means-by-fair-trade.

22.   The name comes from a provision originated in the 19th century in which an exporting country would ask for a commitment to be treated as well as the MFN was treated. That protected the exporting country against later, better deals its partner might strike. In the 1990s debates over trade with China, MFN came to be known as "Normal Trade Relations" to avoid the appearance of calling China a "most-favored nation."

antee, for example, that the United States and Europe would end up with the same levels of auto tariffs, a recently contentious topic.

Through 1961 there were five GATT negotiation rounds.[23] They focused on tariff reductions, steadily lowering average tariff levels among the countries that participated. Between 13 and 38 countries participated in each round. To a large extent, negotiations took place between the economically powerful countries at the center of the trading system—the United States, Japan, Canada, and those in Europe. The results of the negotiations spread to all participants, however, through MFN treatment.

After this initial burst of five rounds in 15 years, the next 35 years featured only three rounds:[24]

- ▶ The Kennedy Round, with 62 countries, 1964–67

- ▶ The Tokyo Round, with 102 countries, 1973–79

- ▶ The Uruguay Round, with 123 countries, 1986–94

The rounds took steadily longer to negotiate each time, included more countries each time, and featured agendas that began to augment tariff discussions with many of the topics discussed in the following chapter such as intellectual property, regulatory barriers, antidumping, and dispute settlement.

The GATT system was at the heart of the global trading system and, by one estimate, delivered benefits to the United States of over $1 trillion per year, or about 10 percent of GDP.[25] The rapidly expanding membership was an additional measure of the system's perceived value. The culminating accomplishment of the late negotiating rounds was the creation of the WTO as the long-awaited institution to govern global trade. The GATT remained as a set of agreements on trade in goods. It was complemented by other agreements such as the General Agreement on Trade in Services, all under the same roof and with a common dispute-settlement mechanism.

---

23. World Trade Organization, "The GATT Years."
24. World Trade Organization, "The GATT Years."
25. Gary Hufbauer and Paul Grieco, "The Payoff from Globalization" (op-ed, Washington, DC: Peterson Institute for International Economics, June 7, 2005), https://piie.com/commentary/op-eds/payoff-globalization.

The developing world

There was a major exception to the requirement for reciprocity under the GATT—the treatment of developing countries.[26] While current political debate in the United States frequently sees developing countries as having an advantage in international competition due to their lower wages or weaker environmental standards, the prevailing view in the 1950s and 1960s was very different.

Developing countries were thought to be at a distinct disadvantage in international competition. Their infrastructure was inferior to that of developed countries. Their workers were measurably less productive than those in developed countries. They had immature, fledgling industries that had to go up against the established industrial giants of the developed world. For much of this time, there were few success stories in developing countries to convince anyone that they had a chance to compete.[27] In fact, some schools of thought described development and dependence traps, in which developing countries would be permanently stuck producing low-value goods, never able to earn enough to invest the capital needed to make higher-value products.[28]

The idea that developing countries were at a distinct disadvantage in the global trading system gave rise to a policy of "special and differential treatment" at the GATT.[29] Under this policy, developing countries were not asked to meet the same requirements as developed countries, including the requirement to engage reciprocally in tariff reduction offers.

It is not clear that this more lenient treatment helped developing countries. It did allow them to maintain high levels of protection and insulate themselves from the global trading system. However, the real success stories—Hong Kong, Korea, Singapore, and Taiwan—were

---

26. See Thirukodikaval Srinivasan, *Developing Countries and the Multilateral Trading System: From GATT to the Uruguay Round and the Future* (Boulder, CO: Westview Press, 2000).

27. Today's success stories looked different back then. In the 1950s, South Korea was poorer than India by almost any measure.

28. For a discussion of dependency theory, see Raúl Prebisch, "Theoretical and Practical Problems of Economic Growth," in *ECLAC Thinking, Selected Texts (1948-1998)*, ed. Ricardo Bielschowsky (Santiago: ECLAC, 2016), 109–28, https://repositorio.cepal.org/handle/11362/43904.

29. "Special and Differential Treatment Provisions," World Trade Organization, https://www.wto.org/english/tratop_e/devel_e/dev_special_differential _provisions_e.htm.

heavily engaged in the global trading system. Further, the principle of reciprocity held *de facto* if not *de jure*. While liberalization had to take place on an MFN basis, the richer, developed countries *could* be selective about the categories of trade in which they would drop barriers. As a result, there was a great deal of liberalization in advanced industrial goods, but much less in agriculture, textiles, or apparel—the sorts of goods that were especially important to developing countries.

In the Uruguay Round, beginning in 1986, developing countries played a more prominent role than they had in any previous negotiation. However, there was a sense among them that they had made concrete commitments in exchange for flimsy promises. In particular, developing countries had committed to trade facilitation measures—sometimes costly policies that would make it less expensive to move goods in and out of the country. In exchange, they had been promised future negotiations on agriculture and liberalization in textiles and apparel. The latter promise was particularly suspect because the liberalization was supposed to take place at the end of a 10-year period, and similar promises to liberalize textile and apparel trade in the past had resulted only in continued protection.

The result of this suspicion was an impasse and a failed meeting to launch a new round in Seattle in 1999.[30] Even in the wake of 9/11, when there was strong global sentiment to address economic concerns through the launch of a new round, developing countries needed to be assured that their concerns would be met. As part of a diplomatic compromise, the result was the Doha Development Agenda launched in Doha, Qatar, in late 2001.[31]

This artful label meant different things to different groups. To the developed countries, it meant they would negotiate reciprocally on issues that were important to developing countries. To developing countries, it meant that others would give, and they would receive.[32]

---

30.   "3 December — The Final Day and What Happens Next," briefing note, World Trade Organization, https://www.wto.org/english/thewto_e/minist_e /min99_e/english/about_e/resum03_e.htm.

31.   *The Road to Doha and Beyond – A Road Map for Successfully Concluding the Doha Development Agenda* (Geneva: World Trade Organization, January 2002).

32.   For a review of this discussion, see Michael J. Finger, "Implementing the Uruguay Round Agreements: Problems for Developing Countries," *The World Economy* 24, no. 9 (September 2001): 1097–108, https://doi.org /10.1111/1467-9701.00402.

The papering over allowed the round to launch. The different views made it very difficult to come to an agreement, even though the suspect promise of textiles and apparel liberalization was, in 2005, fulfilled on schedule.

The Doha talks dragged on until a final, prolonged effort to reach a conclusion came to a head in the summer of 2008 in Geneva. There, the core countries in the negotiations demonstrated what happens when countries do not feel they are receiving reciprocal benefits. Ultimately, the US negotiator, Ambassador Sue Schwab, did not feel offers from India and China were sufficient to match what the United States was putting forward. In particular, she felt that Indian and Chinese demands for flexibility in protecting agriculture would be unacceptable to the US Congress. The session failed, and the Doha talks went largely dormant.

A critical change that helped lead to this failure was the emergence of China as a major trading power (discussed further below). The lenience shown toward developing countries under special and differential treatment was partially based on the idea that those countries were too small to be economically important. China was as poor as other developing countries, but it was neither small nor insignificant.

Bipartisan consensus in the Cold War

There were important shifts over the postwar years in the degree and nature of political support for trade liberalization in the United States. Two important factors, in particular, bolstered the postwar coalition that backed liberalized trade, though both receded over time.

The first was the pre-eminence of the US economy. Unlike the other major economies of the world, the United States emerged from World War II with its economy intact and enjoyed a very strong relative position in the world. According to World Bank data, by 1960 the United States accounted for more than 40 percent of global GDP.[33] Since then, the US economy has more than quintupled in real terms, but the rest of the world grew faster, lowering the US share of global GDP to 24 percent by 2017. Whereas the earlier prowess may have fostered a sense

---

33. The World Bank, "GDP (Current US$)" (data on the world, Washington, DC: The World Bank), https://data.worldbank.org/indicator/NY.GDP.MKTP.CD?end=2017&locations=US-1W&start=1960.

of *noblesse oblige* when it came to opening markets, the sense of relative decline has fostered concerns that the United States is losing.

The second factor involved the Cold War. As I. M. Destler writes,

> [The] move to free trade wasn't just about economics. Trade expansion was central to broader U.S. foreign policy during the Cold War. Together with military alliances, trade agreements helped bind together the major free-market democracies, their growing prosperity serving as an effective counter to the centrally planned economies of the Soviet Bloc and the People's Republic of China.[34]

Trade liberalization was undertaken as a sacrifice, necessary to bind together the countries of the West. In fact, as noted above, the United States grew rapidly, and open markets played a significant role.

Given this sense of free trade as a concession to security requirements, it was not a coincidence that the domestic coalition that supported trade in the United States started to fracture right after the fall of the Berlin Wall in 1989.

At that time, the United States was in the midst of negotiating the Uruguay Round and had just struck an FTA with Canada. Then, in 1990, Mexico approached the United States about negotiating a free trade deal. In fact, the United States had already committed to maintain mostly open markets to Mexico in 1986 when Mexico joined the GATT.[35] Compared to what came next, Mexico's accession to the GATT generated nearly no controversy.

NAFTA

In response to Mexico's request, the George H. W. Bush administration ultimately decided to engage in trilateral talks with Canada and Mexico to create a new NAFTA.[36] The existing trade deal with Canada's and Mexico's GATT accession meant that in 1993, the year before NAFTA

---

34. I. M. Destler, "America's Uneasy History with Free Trade," *Harvard Business Review*, April 28, 2016, https://hbr.org/2016/04/americas-uneasy -history-with-free-trade.

35. "Mexico and the WTO," World Trade Organization, https://www.wto.org /english/thewto_e/countries_e/mexico_e.htm.

36. This section draws on a report for the Atlantic Council. See Phil Levy et al., *What If NAFTA Ended?: The Imperative of a Successful Renegotiation* (Washington, DC: The Atlantic Council, 2017), http://www.atlanticcouncil .org/images/AC_NAFTA_100517_web.pdf.

went into effect, US sectoral tariff rates on Canada and Mexico averaged just 2.7 percent.[37] Given this, one might have expected NAFTA's effects to be minimal. Instead, its implementation in 1994 coincided with a period of burgeoning trade, low unemployment, and strong economic growth in the United States. In the four years following NAFTA, the United States added 800,000 manufacturing jobs—in contrast with the 2 million lost between 1980 and 1993. More broadly, US unemployment averaged 5.1 percent from 1994 to 2007, compared with 7.1 percent from 1982 to 1993.[38]

Yet NAFTA ended up being highly controversial in the United States. It was the first FTA the United States had conducted with a developing country. Mexico had notably lower wages than the United States and less stringent labor and environmental regulations. As NAFTA was being considered during a debate between Ross Perot and Vice President Al Gore, Perot famously predicted that NAFTA would create a "giant sucking sound" as US industry decamped to Mexico.[39] Gore, at the time, countered:

> If low wages were the determinant of where you locate businesses, then Haiti would be an economic powerhouse; Bangladesh would be a powerhouse. We have problems—trade problems—with countries that have wages higher than we have, like Germany, [*sic*] and they have fewer barriers than we do and higher wages because . . . the secret is productivity—our working men and women are the most productive of any nation on the face of the earth.[40]

This did not persuade critics, particularly in organized labor. Clinton had criticized NAFTA's protections for labor and environmental rights as

---

37. Lorenzo Caliendo and Fernando Parro, "Estimates of the Trade and Welfare Effects of NAFTA," NBER Working Paper No. 18508, *Review of Economic Studies* 82, no. 1 (2015): 5. http://doi.org/10.3386/w18508.

38. United States Chamber of Commerce, *NAFTA Triumphant: Assessing Two Decades of Gains in Trade, Jobs, and Growth*, October 27, 2015, https://www.uschamber.com/report/nafta-triumphant-assessing-two-decades-gains-trade-growth-and-jobs.

39. Gary Hufbauer, "Ross Perot Was Wrong About Nafta," *The New York Times*, November 25, 2013, https://www.nytimes.com/roomfordebate/2013/11/24/what-weve-learned-from-nafta/ross-perot-was-wrong-about-nafta.

40. "NAFTA Debate: Gore vs. Perot," *Larry King Live*, CNN, November 9, 1993, http://ggallarotti.web.wesleyan.edu/govt155/goreperot.htm.

insufficient during the 1992 presidential campaign. Upon taking office, Clinton negotiated environmental and labor side letters with Mexico that were meant to address these concerns, but the letters had no real teeth. A central complaint of free trade critics focused on enforcement. Critics argued that commitments in trade agreements were meaningless without an effective mechanism to back them up. NAFTA, as the first US deal with a developing country, became totemic for critics. Decades after NAFTA's 1993 passage, six labor leaders declared:

> Labor is united in its view that NAFTA is a disaster for working people and must be fixed. . . . A new NAFTA must create fair and balanced trade in North America. Real solutions for any new trade deal must dramatically improve workers' rights and raise wages and living standards in all three countries.[41]

The point about balanced trade was closely linked to claims of job loss. The AFL-CIO estimated that between 700,000 and 1 million jobs were lost to NAFTA, a controversial claim repeated by Obama during his 2008 presidential campaign when he promised to withdraw from NAFTA if it were not renegotiated.[42]

As this section opened with data describing US manufacturing job gains in the wake of NAFTA, how can these two claims be reconciled? This is where economic modeling comes in. The job loss claim is based on a problematic multiplier that links trade deficits to job loss, discussed in more detail below. The statistics on job gains can also be problematic in that they do not say what would have happened *without* NAFTA. Perhaps job gains would have been even greater.

There are careful studies that try to estimate the economic impact of NAFTA.[43] They tend to come up with very small, positive numbers for growth and employment. However, such analysis is difficult because the measurable policy change by the United States was very small compared to other economic shocks occurring at the time such as global

---

41. Mark Gruenberg, "Union Leaders to Trump: 'New NAFTA' Must Boost Workers' Rights, Wages," *People's World*, February 22, 2018, http://www.peoplesworld.org/article/union-leaders-to-trump-new-nafta -must-boost-workers-rights-wages.
42. Philip Levy, "Doing a Job on NAFTA," American Enterprise Institute, March 7, 2008, http://www.aei.org/publication/doing-a-job-on-nafta.
43. Caliendo and Parro, "Estimates of the Trade and Welfare Effects of NAFTA."

fiscal policy changes, monetary policy changes, and the completion of the Uruguay Round of the WTO.

NAFTA came into force on January 1, 1994.[44] It was fully phased in by January 1, 2008. Although these are just averages, eliminating 2.7 percent average tariffs over a 14-year period means an average tariff cut of less than 0.2 percent per year. Mexican tariff cuts were much more significant, but Mexico was economically much smaller than the United States at the time NAFTA was signed—roughly 4 percent of the size by GDP, which made it approximately the economic size of Texas.[45]

Of course, NAFTA did more than just cut tariffs. Because Mexico already had nearly duty-free access to the United States before NAFTA, it clearly had other motivations for adopting an agreement that required it to liberalize significantly: Mexico's economic policy had been uneven in the decades leading up to NAFTA. Mexico had adopted reforms, but to draw the desired international investment it needed to persuade investors that the reforms would be lasting. NAFTA served as an effective commitment device.

Mexico and the United States have not always been close. Porfirio Díaz, who served as the president of Mexico a century before NAFTA, is credited with having said: "Poor Mexico, so far from God, so close to the United States."[46] If Mexico were willing to tie its economic fate to its northern neighbor, that was a strong signal to investors that the change was sincere.

This broader partnership was valuable to the United States as well. From an economic perspective, the United States benefited from having

---

44. David Alire and Michael O'Boyle, "The Rocky History of NAFTA," Reuters, September 1, 2017, https://www.reuters.com/article/us-trade-nafta-timeline /the-rocky-history-of-nafta-idUSKCN1BC5IL?il=0.

45. Mexico reduced its average *ad valorem* tariff from 25 percent to 13 percent between 1985 and 1993. See Laurie-Ann Agama and Christine A. McDaniel, "The NAFTA Preference and U.S.-Mexico Trade" (working paper, Office of Economics, United States International Trade Commission, October 2002), https://www.usitc.gov/publications/332/ec200210a.pdf. In 1993, Mexico's average tariff on all imports from the United States was 10 percent, while the US average tariff on all imports from Mexico was 2.07 percent. See Angeles M. Villarreal and Ian F. Fergusson, *The North American Free Trade Agreement (NAFTA)* (Washington, DC: Congressional Research Service, 2014), 5.

46. Rory Carroll, "'So Far from God, So Close to the US': Mexico's Troubled Past with Its Neighbor," *The Guardian*, February 1, 2017, https://www.theguardian.com/us-news/2017/feb/01/donald-trump-us -mexico-relations-history.

Box 1 – GATT Article XXIV: Free trade agreements under the MFN requirement

How could the United States, Canada, and Mexico cut tariffs against each other without extending those tariff cuts to the rest of the world? Would that not be required under GATT rules for MFN treatment?

Actually, the GATT made an exception for FTAs, known as Article XXIV. This says that countries are free from the MFN requirement if they strike an FTA that liberalizes "substantially all trade" and do so in a "reasonable period of time," with a suggestion that 10 years is the longest transition that would count as a reasonable period.

While countries have not always scrupulously followed these conditions, the clause has implications for any potential dissolution of NAFTA. If that were to happen, the United States and Mexico would no longer be able to keep low tariffs under an FTA. Each would be required to impose MFN tariffs on the other. For the United States, the average applied MFN tariff is 3.5 percent. Mexico's average applied MFN tariff is 7 percent.

a prosperous Mexico on its southern border. From a political perspective, NAFTA launched an era of cooperation very different from what had come before, particularly on security issues and in cooperating on immigration.

Contentious bilaterals

In the wake of NAFTA, a sharp partisan divide developed in Congress over trade policy. Many Democrats argued that trade agreements were acceptable only if they had strong, enforceable provisions covering labor and environmental issues. Many Republicans argued that trade agreements were unacceptable if they had such provisions.

Democrats worried that the absence of such provisions would foster a race to the bottom on standards and subject domestic industries to unfair competition. Republicans worried that such provisions were economically unsound—ignoring lower productivity in developing countries—and could be used as a backdoor to stricter labor and environmental regulation in the United States.

One result was that the trade negotiating authority that had been in place since 1975, then known as "fast-track," expired in 1994 and was not renewed under Clinton.[47] While there had been a fairly solid bipartisan pro-trade coalition before NAFTA and before the end of the Cold War, each party still had its protectionists. That made it very difficult to pass new negotiating authority along strictly partisan lines. Without trade negotiating authority, the Clinton administration managed to negotiate only a single, uncontroversial FTA with Jordan.

In 2002 the Bush administration narrowly won TPA by a single vote in the House of Representatives, 215 to 214.[48] The coalition in favor consisted of 194 Republicans and 21 Democrats. Republicans held a majority in the House, so those Democrats replaced 23 Republicans who opposed.

With TPA, the Bush administration set about negotiating FTAs. A first batch of deals included Australia, Chile, and Singapore. These negotiations occurred alongside the early stages of the Doha Development Agenda talks at the WTO. When the Doha talks looked difficult in the fall of 2003, the then US Trade Representative Robert Zoellick sought to expand the network of US FTA partners. This policy—sometimes called "competitive liberalization"—aimed to use bilateral or regional liberalization to spur multilateral liberalization. NAFTA had actually played a somewhat similar role in that it launched in 1990 just as the Uruguay Round of GATT talks faltered. Zoellick was at times criticized for pursuing FTAs with economically small countries (e.g., Bahrain, Oman, and the countries of Central America), but part of the motivation was to introduce developing countries in different regions of the world to the increasingly complex US template for FTAs.

In general, US FTAs built on one another. Provisions of the agreements were described in reference to a predecessor ("NAFTA plus,"

---

47. Juliet Eilperin, "House Defeats Fast-Track Trade Authority," *The Washington Post*, September 26, 1998, https://www.washingtonpost.com/wp-srv/politics/special/trade/stories/fasttrack092698.htm?noredirect=on.

48. Traditionally it has been harder to get trade legislation through the House than the Senate. This may reflect the greater representation of agriculture in the Senate, as the United States is a very successful agriculture exporter. See "H.R. 3005 (107th): Bipartisan Trade Promotion Authority Act of 2002" (data, GovTrack), https://www.govtrack.us/congress/votes/107-2001/h481.

"Chile plus"). The agreements were similar for two reasons. First, they made things easier for US businesses operating under the agreements. Businesses did not need to learn a new set of rules for each trading partner. Second, the agreements facilitated communication with Congress, the equivalent of using "track changes" in a Microsoft Word document. Whether or not it was an actual motivation, the similarity between deals also made it easier to link them together in the future—and to establish a precedent that might be helpful in multilateral negotiations.

Even though the agreements were similar, they evolved over time. In part, this evolution resulted from changes in the economy. When NAFTA was negotiated, for example, there was no such thing as e-commerce. The evolution was also due in part to political shifts.

One such shift took place after the midterm elections of 2006 in which Democrats took control of the House of Representatives. By 2007 when the new Congress was seated, the Bush administration had negotiations concluded or nearing conclusion with Colombia, Panama, Peru, and South Korea. It would need the support of Democrats in the House to pass the agreements. The administration struck a deal with Democrats known as the May 10th Agreement, which notably included new standards for labor, environment, and intellectual property rights for US FTAs.[49] In exchange, the administration thought it had received a promise to get votes on all four pending deals.

However, the only vote permitted was on the Peru FTA, which passed the House in November 2007 and came into force in early 2009.[50] This left Republicans feeling they had not received what had been promised and cast some doubt on whether they ought to adhere to the May 10 terms in future agreements.

The other three agreements languished for years. Obama criticized the agreements when running for office and was not eager to take them

---

49. "Bipartisan Trade Deal," Office of the United States Trade Representative, May 2007, https://ustr.gov/sites/default/files/uploads/factsheets/2007/asset_upload_file127_11319.pdf.
50. "Peru Trade Promotion Agreement," Office of the United States Trade Representative, https://ustr.gov/trade-agreements/free-trade-agreements/peru-tpa.

up. However, his administration tweaked the deals and finally won passage of them in the fall of 2011.[51]

Democrats rebuffed a Republican effort to push for a new TPA at the same time; it had expired in 2007. The politics behind this were understandable. Trade agreements had become highly controversial. Obama had promised to address the concerns of his base by developing new approaches to trade deals, but many of the provisions of trade deals were forged to meet dual concerns of US businesses and trading partners. Breaking that mold risked upsetting either group—or both. Without TPA, Obama could continue to speak of a radically different type of trade agreement. The instructions in the TPA, however, made clear that a new deal would look like a continuing evolution of the old deals. That would have been a politically awkward confession in 2011. Yet the choice would ultimately doom Obama's signature trade project.

TPP

Following a well-established pattern, when the Doha talks under the WTO reached an impasse in the summer of 2008, the United States looked for a regional alternative to multilateral liberalization. The US diagnosis of the problem at the WTO was that major developing countries were not willing to undertake the degree of liberalization that befitted their increasingly prominent place in the global economy. Instead, they were taking advantage of the old norm of special and differential treatment at the WTO and trying to excuse themselves from obligations.

A little over a month after a failed Geneva negotiating session in 2008 that ran into August, US Trade Representative Sue Schwab indicated interest in joining a group of relatively small countries, then known as the P4, in a trade deal they had already partially negotiated and were in the process of upgrading.[52] The point was not the economic draw of the participating countries (Brunei, Chile, New Zealand, and Singapore). In fact, the United States already had FTAs with Chile and Singapore. Rather, the point was to latch onto two key features of

---

51.   As evidence of the minor nature of the changes, none of the "new" deals
      required new negotiating authority or new analyses of economic impact
      by the United States International Trade Commission.
52.   See Claude Barfield and Philip Levy, "Tales of the South Pacific: President
      Obama and the Transpacific Partnership" (Washington, DC: American
      Enterprise Institute for Public Policy Research, December 2009),
      http://www.aei.org/wp-content/uploads/2011/10/09-IEO-Dec-g.pdf.

this "Trans-Pacific Strategic Economic Partnership": an embrace of "high standards" trade agreements and an openness to new members.

"High standards" had become shorthand for the more comprehensive sort of trade agreement that met the demands of modern international commerce. A high-standards agreement dealt not only with tariffs and quotas but with the panoply of issues addressed in the next chapter (financial services, telecommunications, state-owned enterprises, regulatory barriers to trade, government procurement, and so forth).

Although the United States was welcomed by the smaller participants in the existing negotiations, its participation was soon sidelined by the change in administrations. The new Obama administration initially set TPP aside, promising a review. It revived US participation only at the end of 2009 when it discovered the importance that Asian nations placed on their commercial relationship with the United States. In a notably tentative statement delivered in Tokyo, Obama said, "The United States will also be engaging with the Trans-Pacific Partnership countries with the goal of shaping a regional agreement that will have broad-based membership and the high standards worthy of a 21st century trade agreement."[53]

Given subsequent events, it's interesting to consider why it took so long to conclude TPP negotiations. The ultimate deal was reached almost six years later in October 2015 in Atlanta. There are two main reasons: the complexity of the deal and the difficult politics surrounding it.

Modern trade agreements are rarely quick, as there are ample details to work through. TPP covered a broad range of trade topics, including new matters such as electronic commerce for which there was no well-accepted template. Furthermore, in lieu of concluding TPP, the countries involved publicly celebrated the continual expansion of participation. Australia, Peru, and Vietnam announced their intention to join, as the United States had. Malaysia came on in 2010. Canada and Mexico officially joined in 2012. Japan entered in 2013.[54] The presence

---

53. "Remarks by President Barack Obama at Suntory Hall," Office of the Press Secretary, The White House, November 14, 2009, https://obamawhitehouse.archives.gov/the-press-office/remarks-president -barack-obama-suntory-hall.

54. "Timeline of the CPTPP," Government of Canada, last modified December 17, 2018, https://international.gc.ca/trade-commerce/trade-agreements -accords-commerciaux/agr-acc/cptpp-ptpgp/timeline_negotiations -chronologie_negociations.aspx?lang=eng.

of Canada and Mexico meant TPP could serve as a *de facto* update of NAFTA, which passed its two-decade mark shortly after they joined. Japan, as one of the biggest economies in the world, added opportunities and complications.

On top of the inherent complexity of TPP, the Obama administration also took up a matching agreement with Europe, the Trans-Atlantic Trade and Investment Partnership (TTIP). While there was no formal linkage between TPP and TTIP, the Obama trade team tried to coordinate between the two. Particularly on issues such as regulatory commitments and agency practices, for example, it would have been problematic had the two agreements placed conflicting demands on the same agency.

As noted above, TPP negotiations were proceeding in the absence of TPA for the Obama administration. This caused a certain degree of nervousness among the other countries in the negotiations, but the US delegation assured them that it could handle the domestic politics. The plan, evidently, was to conclude all the technical work on the agreement, get TPA from Congress, strike the final political deals among trade ministers, and then submit the deal to Congress.

That might have worked. In late 2013 there was a bipartisan move in Congress to grant President Obama TPA. At the end of the year, a bill emerged from negotiations, known as Camp-Baucus-Hatch for the key congressional leaders who crafted it.[55] Had that bill become law, TPP negotiations could have concluded in late 2014 or early 2015 and the agreement could have come before Congress well before the 2016 general election kicked into high gear.

Instead, the Camp-Baucus-Hatch agreement was dealt two serious blows that proved fatal. First, when Obama delivered his 2014 State of the Union address, he failed to endorse the specific bill that had been negotiated. He called instead for "a bill" giving him TPA authority.

---

55. Rep. Dave Camp (R-MI) was Chairman of the House Ways & Means Committee. Sen. Orrin Hatch (R-UT) was the Ranking Member of the Senate Finance Committee while Sen. Max Baucus (D-MT) was its Chairman.

Second, Obama decided to name Max Baucus ambassador to China, removing the key Democratic sponsor of the legislation.[56]

The political maneuvering meant the next serious attempt to pass TPA did not occur until early summer of 2015. After a tumultuous journey through the House and the Senate—featuring repeated failures—TPA finally passed in late June.[57] While there was a more comfortable margin in the Senate, the bill passed with 218 votes in favor in the House—the bare minimum to ensure a majority.[58] Only 28 House Democrats supported the bill to grant a Democratic president trade negotiating authority.

This was a serious sign of danger for TPP. A vote in favor of TPA meant that a member of Congress was willing to *consider* a trade deal under the specified procedures. It did not guarantee the member's support. On the other hand, a vote against TPA pretty clearly indicated the member would likely not support any outcome to TPP negotiation.

This revealed the extent to which the trade debate had become toxic. The rift was largely along partisan lines, though not entirely: 50 House Republicans opposed TPA, constituting 20 percent of the Republican caucus in the House.

56. This maneuver had serious political implications. Sen. Baucus announced that he would not run again for the Senate. By leaving early for China, the Democratic Governor of Montana could appoint a replacement who could then run in 2014 as an incumbent. Further, Baucus' departure induced a reshuffling of committee chairmanships that left embattled Louisiana Sen. Mary Landrieu as Chairman of the Energy and Natural Resources Committee. Thus, at the cost of slowing the trade agenda, Democrats seemed to increase their odds at holding onto two important seats in a closely divided Senate. In the end, both seats were lost to Republicans in the November 2014 election and Republicans took control of the Senate. See Valerie Volcovici, "Mary Landrieu Set to Take Over Senate Energy Panel Chair," *The Huffington Post*, February 11, 2014, https://www .huffingtonpost.com/2014/02/11/mary-landrieu-senate-energy_n_4770373 .html.

57. Alexander Bolton, "Senate Approves Fast-Track, Sending Trade Bill to White House," *The Hill*, June 24, 2015, http://thehill.com/homenews /senate/246035-senate-approves-fast-track-sending-trade-bill-to-white -house; Phil Levy, "Everything You Need to Know About the Long, Complex Process of Passing the TPA," *Foreign Policy*, June 18, 2015, https://foreignpolicy.com/2015/06/18/everything-you-need-to-know-about -the-impending-death-of-obamas-free-trade-dreams.

58. "H.R. 2146: Defending Public Safety Employees' Retirement Act" (data, GovTrack), https://www.govtrack.us/congress/votes/114-2015/h374.

The Obama administration then found itself in a difficult position. The 2016 general election was fast approaching. Meanwhile, the razor-thin margin of support in Congress left US negotiators little room to maneuver if they hoped to keep the pro-TPA coalition in the House intact for a TPP vote.

TPP countries gathered to try to conclude the deal in late July 2015 in Maui. Those talks failed. They reached a TPP agreement only after contentious negotiations in Atlanta in early October went long past their scheduled deadline.

The conclusion of the deal stirred excitement around the world. Countries in the Asia-Pacific region and beyond that had not been part of the negotiations started thinking about how they might join.

From a US political standpoint, however, the situation looked much grimmer.[59] When the agreement was reached, it commenced the long TPA clock toward ratification. But the delayed conclusion meant that the critical report on TPP's effects on the US economy by the US International Trade Commission (USITC) would not be released until May 2016, relatively late in the presidential primary season.[60] By that time, both Hillary Clinton and Donald Trump had declared their opposition to the deal.[61]

The agreement was never submitted to Congress. There was talk of a lame-duck strategy to pass the agreement after the November election, but that ultimately did not succeed, given both the result of the election and the failure of the Obama administration to build a bigger coalition in favor of the deal. One of President Trump's first acts upon taking office was to pull the United States out of the deal.[62]

---

59. Phil Levy, "Did Obama's Trade Agenda Just Quietly Run Out of Time?" *Foreign Policy*, August 3, 2015, https://foreignpolicy.com/2015/08/03/did-obamas-trade-agenda-just-quietly-run-out-of-time.

60. There was no eagerness on the part of Congress to take up TPP before its likely effects had been studied. This same reluctance was evident in 2018 when House Speaker Paul Ryan (R-WI) gave a May deadline for concluding NAFTA renegotiation talks. The 105 days for the USITC to assess the deal were regarded as inviolate.

61. Adam Taylor, "A Timeline of Trump's Complicated Relationship with the TPP," *The Washington Post*, April 13, 2018, https://www.washingtonpost.com/news/worldviews/wp/2018/04/13/a-timeline-of-trumps-complicated-relationship-with-the-tpp/?utm_term=.521118af09d9.

62. "Trump Executive Order Pulls Out of TPP Trade Deal," BBC, January 24, 2017, https://www.bbc.com/news/world-us-canada-38721056.

This might have seemed the end of the story. But it potentially marks the beginning of a new phase of US trade history—one in which the United States is on the outside looking in as other countries write global trade rules. In the wake of the US departure from TPP, the remaining countries rechristened it the Comprehensive and Progressive Trans-Pacific Partnership, suspended 22 parts of the agreement that had been there solely for the benefit of the United States, and passed the new deal in March 2018. The concluding chapter of this monograph will consider the implications should the United States decide to relinquish its long-standing role as a leader in trade liberalization.

Before moving on from TPP, though, it is worth asking why it became such a focus of scorn. It would be tempting to call it divisive, yet it actually seemed to heal a long-standing partisan rift and unite Democrats and Republicans in opposition, albeit for different reasons.[63]

There are at least two explanations for why TPP was so controversial despite fitting easily into the tradition of US trade agreements. Each will be explored at some length in ensuing sections of the monograph.

First, the expansion of the negotiating agenda that had begun during GATT rounds in the 1970s and 1980s culminated in a very broad set of negotiating topics for TPP. These topics stretched well beyond the traditional "border issues" of tariffs and quotas. In the heat of the 2016 general election, the distinguished economist Jeffrey D. Sachs wrote:

> I am a believer in expanded international trade, but I am an opponent of TPP and TTIP. This isn't a contradiction. . . . The proposed treaties are more than trade agreements. They would also establish many important rules of the economy beyond trade, and in fact would give far too much power to large multinational companies, the corporations whose lobbyists have helped to draft the agreements.[64]

Such opposition centered on both the manner in which the negotiations took place and on the nature of the new negotiating agenda. Whereas economists largely agree about the effects of tariffs or quotas, there is no similar consensus about the ideal length of time for patent protection

---

63. This is opposition at the level of national political leadership. In public opinion polls, TPP had majority support.

64. Jeffrey D. Sachs, "The Truth about Trade," *The Boston Globe*, October 17, 2016, https://www.bostonglobe.com/opinion/2016/10/16/the-truth-about-trade/UWtu8jpAo8LTsTFlffaZOK/story.html.

(intellectual property) or the appropriate legal rights of foreign investors (investor protections). This critique was intimately tied to the details of TPP and similar agreements. The next chapter will consider the panoply of new issues that have proven so controversial.

The second major cause of opposition was concern about the negative impact of trade on certain segments of the population—the *losers* from trade. International trade courses have taught for decades that trade liberalization *can* create winners and losers.[65] There is a logical addendum that often gets lost in the discussion, however: just because a worker has been disadvantaged does not mean he or she was disadvantaged by trade alone. This critique tends to have relatively little to do with the details of the agreements. The agreements instead played a more totemic role as symbols of a deeper discontent. This was particularly true for the alleged demise of American manufacturing, which is the subject of the next section.

Manufacturing

As the global postwar trading system was developing, the US economy was evolving as well. By 2015 more than 75 percent of US economic output was in the service sector.[66] Much of the developed world saw this kind of growth in the service sector. The figure is similar for the entire Organisation for Economic Co-operation and Development (OECD) club of high-income economies.[67] While the service sector often evokes images of someone flipping burgers at a fast food restaurant, it encompasses activities as diverse as healthcare, banking, transportation, entertainment, and computer programming.

---

65. The two canonical arguments are: (1) The Stolper-Samuelson theorem, which argues that trade liberalization will disadvantage the relatively scarce factor in an economy and help the relatively abundant factor (e.g., in the United States, help capital and hurt labor) and (2) A "specific factors" model, in which factors of production that cannot move between sectors will see their returns fall when trade drives down the price of the good in that sector.

66. The World Bank, "Services, Value Added (% of GDP)" (data on the United States, Washington, DC: The World Bank), https://data.worldbank.org/indicator/NV.SRV.TOTL.ZS?locations=US.

67. The World Bank, "Services, Value Added (% of GDP)" (data on the United States and the OECD members, Washington, DC: The World Bank), https://data.worldbank.org/indicator/NV.SRV.TOTL.ZS?locations=US-OE.

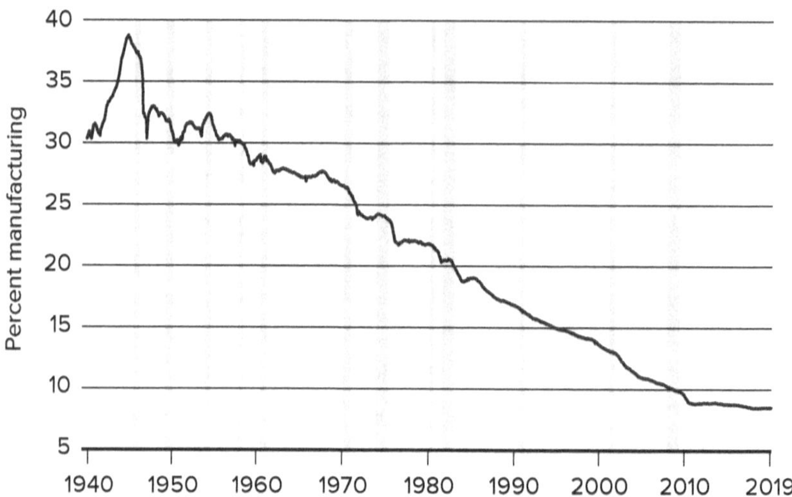

Source: US Bureau of Labor Statistics, retrieved from FRED, Federal Reserve Bank of St. Louis, February 13, 2019, https://fred.stlouisfed.org/series /MANEMP.

Nonetheless, manufacturing maintains a grip on the popular imagination and has played a disproportionate role in discussions of trade policy. Trump, on the campaign trail in 2016, said NAFTA had "destroyed our manufacturing in this country."[68] This dire assessment is based on the decline of overall jobs in the US manufacturing sector. Figure 1 shows the share of US nonfarm jobs in the manufacturing sector.

Indeed, this figure seems to paint a picture of decline. From a World War II peak of nearly 40 percent employment in manufacturing, the share plunges to its current level of less than 9 percent. Beginning around the mid-1960s, this decline appears almost uninterrupted. There are little ups and downs—the gray vertical bars show recessions, which almost invariably cause dips in the manufacturing sector—but the trend is reasonably consistent.

The timing of this decline poses a challenge for a story in which trade agreements such as NAFTA destroy American manufacturing. As noted above, NAFTA and the creation of the WTO both occurred in the

---

68. Robert Farley, "Trump on the Stump," FactCheck.org, September 28, 2016, https://www.factcheck.org/2016/09/trump-on-the-stump.

Figure 2 – US manufacturing real output

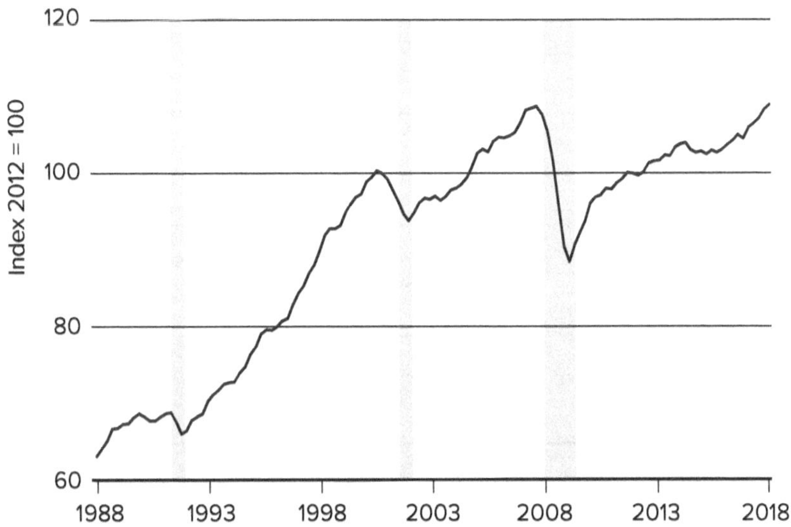

Source: US Bureau of Labor Statistics, retrieved from FRED, Federal Reserve Bank of St. Louis, February 13, 2019, https://fred.stlouisfed.org/series /OUTMS.

mid-1990s. By that time the decline had been under way for decades. There is no notable downturn that accompanies their entry into force. Similarly, China's accession to the WTO was in 2001. By that point manufacturing had declined to roughly 12 percent of the workforce, fairly close to its current level. It is difficult to suggest that these trade policies caused the manufacturing decline if the decline came first.

Still, the puzzle of the decline of the manufacturing sector remains. Figure 2 shows US manufacturing *real output*—the amount of goods the manufacturing sector produced (controlling for inflation).

This graph, which covers a shorter time period, tells a very different story. Real output in the first quarter of 2018 was 68 percent higher than in the first quarter of 1987 (the earliest data available for this series). This does not seem to be a story of failure. In fact, other data support that interpretation. In 2017, the latest year for which data are available, the WTO ranks the United States as the number two exporter of mer-

Figure 3 – US manufacturing real output per worker

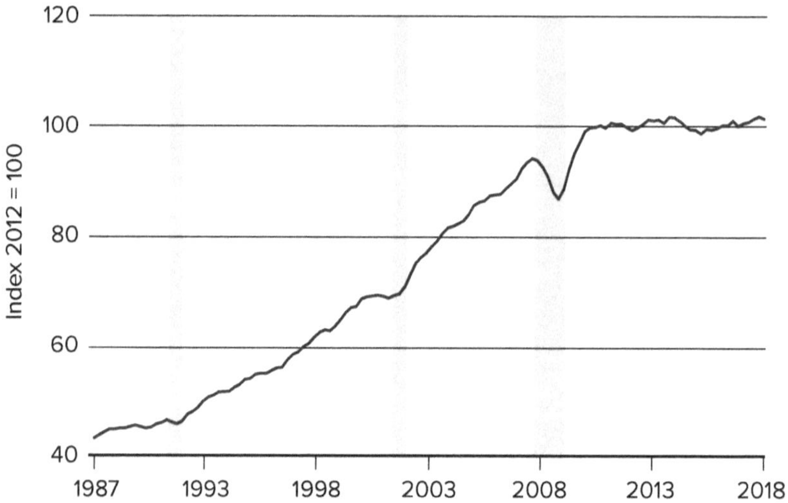

Source: US Bureau of Labor Statistics, retrieved from FRED, Federal Reserve Bank of St. Louis, February 13, 2019, https://fred.stlouisfed.org/series /PRS30006163.

chandise in the world, behind only China.[69] The United States shipped $1.545 trillion in goods, accounting for 8.7 percent of global merchandise exports.[70] This is hardly a country whose manufacturing sector has been destroyed.

To understand what happened, a third perspective is helpful. Figure 3 combines the two previous trends by looking at real output *per worker*. The figure shows a sector with a productivity boom, albeit one that seemed to end in 2010. From 1987 to 2010, output per person grew by roughly 130 percent. The manufacturing sector turned out more goods with fewer people.

This reflects the rise of automation in the manufacturing sector. There is no longer a need for workers to carry palettes across the factory floor. Such tasks can be done by robots or conveyor belts.

---

69. World Trade Organization, "International Trade and Market Access Data," https://www.wto.org/english/res_e/statis_e/statis_bis_e.htm?solution =WTO&path=/Dashboards/MAPS&file=Map.wcdf&bookmarkState ={%22impl%22:%22client%22,%22params%22:{%22langParam%22:%22en %22}}.
70. World Trade Organization, "International Trade and Market Access Data."

Rather, workers now need the skills to program computer-guided machine tools.

In fact, machine tools offer two keys to help understand the perception of American manufacturing failure. First, the demand for manufacturing workers with technical skills exacerbates the impact of the employment decline. This sector used to provide an avenue for someone with limited education or "low skills" to attain a middle-class lifestyle through hard work. Today, not only have the number of jobs decreased, but the remaining jobs often demand at least a couple years of supplementary training beyond high school. From the perspective of once-strong, blue-collar communities, this looks like the closing of an important avenue to prosperity.

The second insight offered by machine tools concerns *what* the United States produces. In 2017 the top broad category of US exports in goods was "capital goods," which totaled $533 billion.[71] Along with machine tools, this category includes items such as industrial machines, civilian aircraft, semiconductors, and telecommunications equipment. The next biggest export category was "industrial supplies," which totaled $465 billion in exports in 2017. This includes petroleum, plastics, and chemicals.

By definition, these are not household items. The kinds of products the average shopper sees in a big-box store go under the category "consumer goods." That was the second biggest category of *imports* into the United States in 2017, valued at $602 billion. When people focus on the kinds of goods they consume (e.g., toys, appliances, and televisions), they develop the misleading impression that the United States no longer makes anything.

But if consumer goods was only the second-biggest import category into the United States, what was the first? Capital goods was first, the same category that led the export list. This highlights two important trends that have reshaped manufacturing trade in the last several decades: *intra-industry trade* and *global value chains*. Intra-industry trade refers to the idea that the United States and another country (say, Germany) might ship machine tools to each other. This challenges the idea of comparative advantage. Shouldn't one of the two countries have

---

71. Bureau of Economic Analysis, US Department of Commerce, "U.S. International Trade in Goods and Services November 2018," news release CB 19-05, BEA 19-02, February 6, 2019, https://www.bea.gov/system /files/2019-02/trad1118_4.pdf.

a comparative advantage in machine tools, and shouldn't production concentrate there?

In fact, intra-industry trade offers a complementary explanation for international trade. Even if the United States and Germany are equally good at producing machine tools, each may want to specialize in producing one *type* of machine tool. This makes sense when there are large fixed costs to setting up a machine tool factory (or an auto or semiconductor plant). Rather than the countries incurring the large fixed cost multiple times, each can specialize in certain types of machine tools and send the varieties back and forth. This type of trade has played a significant role in the enormous expansion of trade in the postwar era. It also helps explain why the United States imports goods that it can technically make at home.

Dividing up production around the globe to cut costs is not limited to complete production processes. It also applies to the various stages of producing complex goods such as autos, aircraft, or smartphones. This process of divvying up production stages has created global value chains, having several important implications for trade in manufactures.

First, global value chains mean that countries can be competitive making products that would otherwise be too costly to produce. Second, they mean that the distinction between importing and exporting companies has seriously blurred. Figure 4 illustrates this relationship. The firm-level data in the United States show that top US exporters are often heavy importers—and vice versa.

The final major implication of global value chains in manufacturing concerns the effects of interruptions in trade, whether by tariff or natural disaster. When Japan was hit by the Fukushima earthquake and tsunami in 2011, it did more than sideline some Japanese car production. It shook assembly lines around the world since the affected region of Japan was producing specialized paint, auto transmissions, and semiconductors used in car factories elsewhere.[72]

While the manufacturing sector still resonates in the public imagination, it has transformed significantly over the last 70 years. The global trend toward more capital-intensive techniques—making more goods with fewer people—has resulted in fewer manufacturing jobs and changed the skill requirements for those jobs that remain.

---

72.   Jamie Page Deaton, "What the Disaster in Japan Means for Car Buyers Here," U.S. News and World Report, March 29, 2011, https://cars.usnews.com/cars-trucks/what-the-disaster-in-japan-means-for-car-buyers-here.

Figure 4 – Types of exporters and importers

Top 1% of US exporters
(2,000 firms)

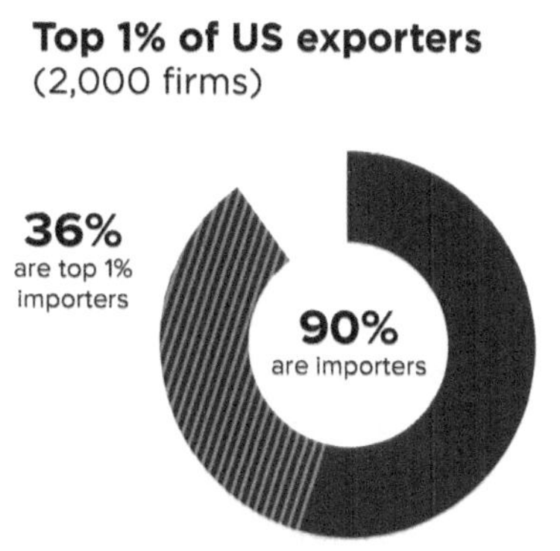

Top 1% of US importers
(1,300 firms)

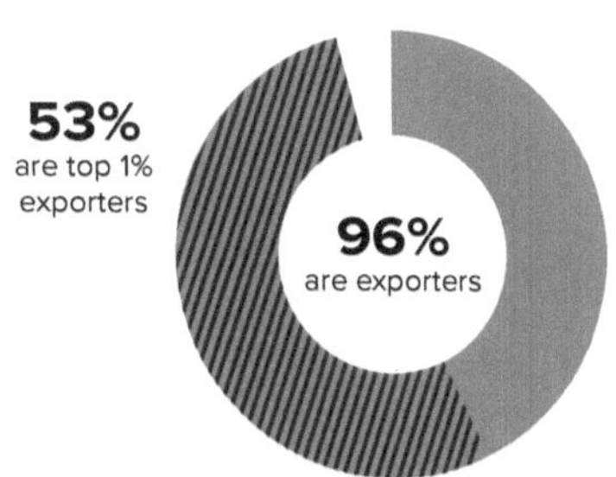

▸ Account for 66% of US
goods import
▸ Employed 14 million (2007; same
as manufacturing sector in that year)

▸ Account for 66% of US
goods exports
▸ Employed 13 million (2007)

Source: "Importers are Exporters: Tariffs Would Hurt Our Most Competitive Firms," *Trade & Investment Policy Watch*, December 7, 2016, by J. Bradford Jensen, Peterson Institute for International Economics, https://piie.com /blogs/trade-investment-policy-watch/importers-are-exporters-tariffs-would -hurt-our-most-competitive.

International trade has certainly played some role in this transformation, but not the predominant one that many imagine.[73] Labor-intensive plants closed in the United States at the same time that the parent companies opened new facilities in Mexico or China. But there were also new plant openings in the United States that bolstered overall manufacturing output. However, those new plants were often in different parts of the country with less expensive labor and more automated production systems.

China in the global trading system

For those who blame trade and globalization for modern-day social ills, no country appears as culpable as the People's Republic of China. Its years of double-digit economic growth have vaulted it to the top of the world's export tables and given the impression that it is an unstoppable

---

73. Michael Hicks and Srikant Devaraj, *The Myth and the Reality of Manufacturing in America* (Muncie, IN: Ball State University, June 2015 and April 2017), https://conexus.cberdata.org/files/MfgReality.pdf.

behemoth. Its heavy state involvement in economic affairs has both convinced critics that China does not play fair and aroused suspicion that political motives are behind its investments and activities. China's aggressive approach to acquiring intellectual property and its role as a base from which cyberattacks are launched have only exacerbated these suspicions.[74]

Amid China's economic emergence, its role in the global trading system is the subject of heated debate. Those debates have intensified in recent years as China integrated further into world trade flows. To set the stage for the current debates, it is worth going back to see when China's resurgence started.

From the mid-1960s into the 1970s, China was in the throes of the Cultural Revolution, a wrenching political upheaval that left the Chinese economy in shambles. By 1980 China's annual output per person was a measly $195 in current terms, just over 50 cents per day, and only 1.5 percent of the US level (see figure 5).[75] China was a poor, isolated country, albeit a very large one.

In the wake of the Cultural Revolution, China adopted several policy changes that would set the course for its emergence as a trading power over the decades that followed. First, in the midst of the Cultural Revolution, China reestablished political relations with the United States, beginning with President Richard Nixon's visit with Mao Zedong. Second, this political opening was followed by a gradual, tentative economic opening under Mao's successor, Deng Xiaoping. Finally, China adopted a "one-child" policy that mostly limited Chinese families to having only one child. While the impact of the economic policy changes may seem more obvious, the demographic policy had serious repercussions that persist today. With the ravages of the Cultural Revolution and the travails that preceded it, China had a limited elderly population.[76] Combined with the one-child policy, which limited the youth population, China had created a population bulge that, within a decade or two,

---

74. Dorothy Denning, "Cyberwar: How Chinese Hackers Became a Major Threat to the U.S.," *Newsweek*, October 5, 2017, https://www.newsweek .com/chinese-hackers-cyberwar-us-cybersecurity-threat-678378.

75. The World Bank, "GDP per Capita (Current US$)" (data on China and the United States, Geneva: The World Bank), https://data.worldbank.org /indicator/NY.GDP.PCAP.CD?locations=CN-US.

76. "China 1980," PopulationPyramid.net, https://www.populationpyramid.net /china/1980.

Figure 5 – China output per person (US dollars)

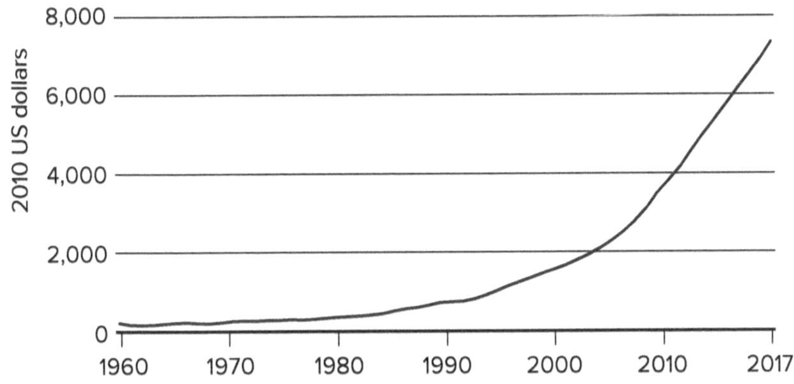

Source: World Bank, retrieved from FRED, Federal Reserve Bank of St. Louis, February 13, 2019, https://fred.stlouisfed.org/series/NYGDPPCAPKDCHN.

would reach prime working age and pass through that stage over a period of decades.

At an elementary level, there are two broad ways a country can grow quickly: it can rapidly accumulate key inputs for economic production, and it can use inputs more productively.[77] China's favorable demographic bulge accompanied the possibility of catching up with the rest of the world in productivity. As a bonus, China enjoyed highly favorable geography—it sat at the heart of fast-growing East Asian economies and could tap into their supply chains. This meant, for example, that China did not initially need to produce all the parts of a computer. It could begin with relatively low-skilled assembly and build out from there. The result was extraordinarily rapid economic growth.

---

77. For more sophisticated and careful explanations of China's growth and productivity history, see Chang-Tai Hsieh and Peter J. Klenow, "Misallocation and Manufacturing TFP in China and India," *The Quarterly Journal of Economics* 124, no. 4 (2009): 1403–48. Also see Loren Brandt, Debin Ma, and Thomas G. Rawski, "From Divergence to Convergence: Reevaluating the History Behind China's Economic Boom," *Journal of Economic Literature* 52, no. 1 (2014): 45–123, http://doi.org/10.1257/jel.52.1.45. Finally, see Xiaodong Zhu, "Understanding China's Growth: Past, Present, and Future," *Journal of Economic Perspectives* 26, no. 4 (2012): 103–24, http://doi.org/10.1257/jep.26.4.103.

The driving forces of Chinese economic growth would not support the idea of China as juggernaut. Just as Western concern about Chinese dominance surged, China's economic growth began to reach its limits. Today, China faces a dire "graying" of its population as workers age and are not replaced by youth.[78] China's working-age population began falling in 2014, a trend that appears will continue.[79] Once a country like China catches up to Western productivity levels, it will face the same innovation challenges as the West. It is significantly more difficult to push out the frontiers of knowledge than to catch up to the state of the art.

The prospect of a shrinking workforce, rising wages, an aging population, and the need to innovate all plague China's leadership. Meanwhile, China's growth has raised its per-capita income to just under $9,000. That contrasts with almost $59,500 for the United States.[80] In the context of trade policy, this helps explain a striking disconnect in worldview between China and some of its critics. While the critics see a world-beating juggernaut, the Chinese see their nation as a still-developing country with manifold challenges.

During the era when China was largely shut off from the world, the United States maintained moderately high trade barriers toward China, as it had against most communist countries. This policy, formalized by the Jackson-Vanik Amendment in 1975, denied such countries MFN status.[81]

Then, when China began to open to the world, the United States reciprocated with a grant of MFN status, permitted by a presidential waiver of Jackson-Vanik. Recent political discourse—and even some academic literature—gives the impression that this opening took place when China was permitted to join the WTO. In fact, it was more than 20 years earlier in October 1979. China has enjoyed MFN trade status from

---

78. Nicholas Eberstadt, "The Demographic Future: What Population Growth—and Decline—Means for the Global Economy," *Foreign Affairs* 89, no. 6 (2010): 54–64, http://www.jstor.org/stable/20788716.
79. Reuters, "China Working-Age Population Shrinks, Presenting Pitfall for Pension Plans," Reuters, February 28, 2018, https://www.reuters.com /article/us-china-economy-population/china-working-age-population -shrinks-presenting-pitfall-for-pension-plans-idUSKCN1GC18C.
80. The World Bank, "GDP Per Capita (Current US$)."
81. See William H. Cooper, *The Jackson-Vanik Amendment and Candidate Countries for WTO Accession: Issues for Congress* (Washington, DC: Congressional Research Service, July 26, 2012), https://fas.org/sgp/crs /row/RS22398.pdf.

the United States ever since—even through the Tiananmen Square protests in 1989 and Clinton's pledge to revoke MFN status in his successful 1992 presidential campaign.[82]

The confusion on this point arises because China's absence from the GATT meant that the United States maintained the *option* to revoke China's MFN status. It was only when China joined the WTO in December 2001 that the United States was obliged to accord MFN status. During the decades that the United States retained the option, Congress attempted to revoke China's MFN status on numerous occasions. As this was before China had grown to its present size, most congressional debates concerned China's human rights record rather than its economic impact. Nonetheless, through Republican and Democratic presidencies and across changes in control of the House and the Senate, the persistent judgment was that the United States was better off engaging with China than attempting to isolate it.

China applied to become a member of the GATT as early as July 1986. As one analyst noted, that made it "easily . . . the longest and most arduous accession negotiation in the history of the GATT/WTO."[83] The difficulty largely stemmed from a fundamental disagreement over how China should be treated. The Chinese view was that China was a poor, developing country and should, therefore, be saddled with the minimal obligations that the GATT traditionally accorded to developing countries. The major powers of the GATT, however, saw China as sufficiently large enough to require more serious reform before it could be admitted. In the end, China made substantial reform commitments through its Protocol of Accession.

While substantial, these commitments did not require China to eliminate all subsidies to industry nor to rid itself of state-owned enterprises. That was because *no* WTO member was required to implement that level of free-market reform. WTO rules were not about mandating idealized behavior. Rather, they represented a compromise among members who had their own subsidies and interventions they wished to preserve. In the same vein, while China committed to dramatically reduce its tar-

---

82.   "Clinton and China: How Promise Self-Destructed," *The New York Times*, May 29, 1994, https://www.nytimes.com/1994/05/29/world/clinton-and -china-how-promise-self-destructed.html.

83.   Jeffrey Gertler, *What China's WTO Accession Is All About* (Washington, DC: The World Bank, December 14, 2002), http://siteresources.worldbank .org/INTRANETTRADE/Resources/Gertler.pdf.

iffs upon joining the WTO, the tariffs were not eliminated—a standard case for almost all WTO members. Further, China joined the WTO at the launch of the Doha negotiations, when the expectation was that new rules would soon be forthcoming.

Yet China was unlike other WTO members in many ways, and its Protocol of Accession recognized this. Among its extensive provisions, it declared that other WTO members could treat China as a "nonmarket economy" for 15 years after it joined. In practice, this made it substantially easier to apply tariffs against China for selling goods too cheaply (antidumping) or with subsidized prices (countervailing duties). Recently, this provision became contentious. China originally interpreted the rule to say that, after the specified 15 years, it would be considered a "market economy." Europe and the United States had a different interpretation: when the late 2016 date rolled around, they claimed they were only required to reevaluate China's status, not automatically accord it market economy status.[84] China filed a complaint with the WTO, which is still being adjudicated.

There have been two main lines of complaint about China's economic behavior since it joined the WTO. The first involves currency and trade balances. The second involves the economic impact of trade with China on US labor markets. In each case, some important details have been lost in the heat of the debates.

On currency and trade balances, China pegged its currency at 8.28 renminbi to the dollar from 1994.[85] This was a fairly standard practice for a country with doubts about its monetary policy. It effectively outsourced the determination of the money supply to the United States. This meant that China's current account balance with the world fluctuated in a normal range until about 2003.[86] China held its currency fixed

---

84. Wayne M. Morrison, "China's Status as a Nonmarket Economy (NME)," news release IFI0385, Congressional Research Service, January 10, 2019, https://fas.org/sgp/crs/row/IF10385.pdf.

85. Elvis Picardo, "Why China's Currency Tangos with the USD," Investopedia, February 12, 2014, https://www.investopedia.com/articles/forex/09/chinas -peg-to-the-dollar.asp.

86. The current account balance is not identical to the trade balance, but it is close enough. See J. B. Maverick, "What Is the Difference Between a Current Account Deficit and a Trade Deficit?" Investopedia, January 25, 2018, https://www.investopedia.com/ask/answers/010715/what -difference-between-current-account-deficit-and-trade-deficit.asp.

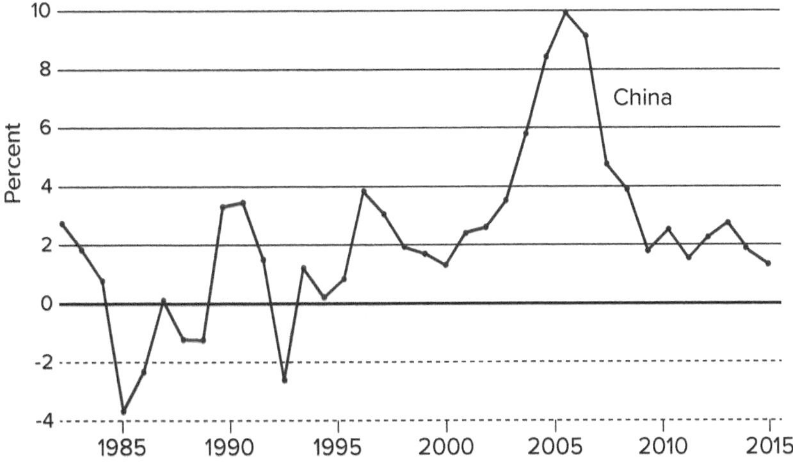

Source: International Monetary Fund, Balance of Payments Statistics Year-
book and data files, and World Bank and OECD GDP estimates.

to the dollar even during the Asian financial crisis, when many countries
in the region depreciated their currencies.

Then, two notable things happened. First, China's *bilateral* trade balance with the United States shot up. Then its current account with the
world ballooned to almost 10 percent of GDP in 2007. The US move was
a bit of a head fake since bilateral trade balances have no economic
meaning (discussed in "Trade balances" below). Nonetheless, it drew a
strong political reaction from the United States since the global imbalance became more significant as China grew into a major player. The
two moves in combination drew charges of "currency manipulation" and
outcries that China was stealing US jobs.

In fact, China began to appreciate its currency in 2005, shortly after
the global imbalance became clear and after it had made the arrangements it saw as necessary.[87] It appreciated its currency slowly—between
5 and 10 percent each year—which did not appease critics. Yet in a
recurring theme with China policy, those critics rarely proposed a better

---

87.   Given China's long-standing fixed currency, it did not initially have any for-
       ward currency markets. That meant its export businesses could not initially
       take the sort of precautions against currency swings that were common in
       more developed financial markets.

alternative.[88] If China had floated its currency, it might have depreciated. If it had tried to appreciate its currency rapidly, it would have invited economic disaster.

As it was, the appreciation, combined with the global financial crisis, brought China's current account surplus down quickly. By 2011 it was under 2 percent.

The second main line of complaint concerns the effect of trade with China on US labor markets. This became known as the "China Shock" literature.[89] Although academics had been scornful of the focus on trade balances—particularly bilateral ones—they embraced this new argument as showing that trade with China had particularly damaged local US labor markets in the 2000s.

There are two major problems with this research.[90] First, it is not clear what shock they are measuring. One paper explicitly looks at China's WTO accession, but this did not mark a policy change.[91] Second, it is not clear in the literature what the counterfactual might be. Is it that China somehow disappears from the earth? Or that it somehow keeps trading with every country but the United States? And what would hap-

---

88. *China's Exchange Rate Policy: Hearing Before the Committee on Ways and Means, U.S. House of Representatives*, 111th Cong., 2nd Sess. (March 24, 2010) (statement of Philip I. Levy, PhD, Resident Scholar, The American Enterprise Institute), https://www.govinfo.gov/content/pkg/CHRG-111hhrg 63077/pdf/CHRG-111hhrg63077.pdf.

89. The two most notable lines of work here are as follows: David H. Autor, David Dorn, and Gordon H. Hanson, "The China Syndrome: Local Labor Market Effects of Import Competition in the United States," *American Economic Review* 103, no. 6 (October 2013): 2121–68, https://www.aeaweb .org/articles?id=10.1257/aer.103.6.2121; Justin R. Pierce and Peter K. Schott, "The Surprisingly Swift Decline of US Manufacturing Employment," *American Economic Review* 106, no. 7 (July 2016): 1632–62, https://www.aeaweb.org/articles?id=10.1257/aer.20131578.

90. Philip Levy, "Did China Trade Cost the United States 2.4 Million Jobs?" *Foreign Policy*, May 8, 2016, https://foreignpolicy.com/2016/05/08 /did-china-trade-cost-the-united-states-2-4-million-jobs.

91. The paper argues that US investors were poised, waiting to be hit by non-MFN China tariffs for 20 years, and only reacted once the threat formally lifted. The implausible part is that, under this construction, investors not only needed to be worried about China tariffs for two decades, they had to be worried in exact proportion to the Smoot-Hawley tariffs that would apply to their industry. It is highly unlikely that any investors *knew* what their Smoot-Hawley tariffs were. When non-MFN tariffs were ultimately proposed by Trump in the 2016 campaign, they were 45 percent across the board. They had nothing to do with Smoot-Hawley.

pen in neighboring countries, such as Vietnam, that were starting to underprice China by the end of the 2000s?

However misguided, the China Shock literature has nonetheless lent credence to political arguments that trade with China has been uniquely harmful. As one result, the Office of the US Trade Representative concluded in a 2017 report that it had been a mistake to admit China to the WTO.[92] As with the academic literature, the report did not suggest any policy available at the time that might have been superior.[93]

The problematic nature of these prominent China critiques hardly absolves Chinese behavior. Instead, it has served to cloud an already difficult debate. There are serious concerns about Chinese political and economic behavior. The latter include a more recent trend in which China has backed away from market-oriented reforms, retained a prominent role for state-owned enterprises, and engaged in serious attempts to coerce intellectual property from Western companies.

The major challenge for the United States will be to decide whether to work with China to craft a role in which China is a "responsible stakeholder" in the global economic system or to try to isolate China economically. The former is likely to prove difficult, the latter impossible.

Conclusion

The current trade frictions have multiple roots: the response to the protectionist mistakes of the Great Depression; the transformation of manufacturing amid technological change and global supply chains; and the emergence of China as a trading power. History helps us understand the policy questions that are currently being posed. As one considers a reworking of the trade system, an understanding of the past can help clarify which elements are there for a reason and should be retained.

The actual reworking of trade policy, however, quickly moves from grand schemes and visions to specific policies and questions. As noted above, the set of policies under consideration has expanded dramatically over the years. The next chapter looks at old standards up through some of the newer and more controversial items on the agenda.

---

92.   United States Trade Representative, *2017 Report to Congress on China's WTO Compliance* (Washington, DC: Office of the United States Trade Representative, January 2018), https://ustr.gov/sites/default/files/files /Press/Reports/China%202017%20WTO%20Report.pdf.

93.   Levy, "Did China Trade Cost the United States 2.4 Million Jobs?"

Chapter III: What are the issues?

Introduction: Tariffs and market access

In the beginning, there were tariffs. That may be a bit of an overstatement, but tariffs are the granddaddy of all trade measures. For centuries they were used as an important means of collecting government revenue. Even when it was difficult to collect income or sales taxes, it was possible to put taxes on imports. Frequently, for young or developing countries, a large portion of consumption needs would be imported through a key port or two. This made taxation easier.

A tariff is simply a tax on imports. For example, it could require that anyone purchasing a horizontal lathe from China for $6,000 pay a 25 percent tariff, which would mean an additional $1,500 paid to the US government.[94] That tax—or "duty"—is collected by US Customs and Border Protection. Lathe imports were, in fact, part of the first batch of $34 billion in Chinese imports hit with tariffs in the summer of 2018.[95]

At first glance, this would seem to be a small vindication of President Trump's claim that tariffs would result in "big dollars . . . flowing into our Treasury."[96] Before celebrating, it is worth asking who pays that tariff—or whether it gets paid at all.

The question of who pays a tariff depends on the nature of the world market. If the United States were the only market for Chinese lathes and the Chinese were committed to selling them at any price, then it could be the case that the Chinese manufacturers will swallow the cost of the

---

94. "Ck6432 High Precision Small Flat Bed Horizontal Metal CNC Lathe," Focus Technology, https://lycncmachine.en.made-in-china.com/product/fKNEYzPAOLUF/China-Ck6432-High-Precision-Small-Flat-Bed-Horizontal-Metal-CNC-Lathe.html.

95. United States Trade Representative, *Section 301 Enforcements and List, China 2018* (Washington, DC: Office of the United States Trade Representative), https://ustr.gov/sites/default/files/enforcement/301Investigations/List%201.pdf.

96. John Bowden, "Trump Defends Tariffs: When We Use Them 'Foolish People Scream!'" *The Hill*, August 4, 2018, https://thehill.com/policy/finance/trade/400404-trump-defends-tariffs-when-we-use-them-foolish-people-scream.

tariff. They had hoped to earn $6,000 without the tariff, but will instead take home only $4,500.

What if, instead, there were multiple countries that bought lathes, such as Australia, Canada, Japan, and members of the European Union? If $6,000 was the going price, a lathe manufacturer in China could choose where to ship its product. If US consumers offered anything less than a net $6,000, the manufacturer would just collect the full price elsewhere. In this case, the $1,500 tariff would have to be paid by the US importing company—a tax on an American business. Instead of a machine costing $6,000, they would pay a total of $7,500, putting them at a notable disadvantage compared to their manufacturing rivals in other countries.

So far, we have been assuming that the Chinese lathe sale to the United States goes through despite the tariff. But it need not. If the manufacturer decides to sell the lathe somewhere else, or if the importer decides to buy from a different country, or if either decides they cannot make money at those prices, then there will be no transaction. No transaction, no tariff revenue.[97] The higher the tariffs, the more likely the purchasing deal is called off. This gives the somewhat counterintuitive result that higher tariffs can mean less revenue.[98]

Why do domestic companies push for tariffs? Because they can raise prices. If you are a domestic producer of steel rods, for example, you are limited in the price you can charge customers by the threat that, if you charge too much, they will turn instead to foreign suppliers.[99] If tariffs raise the price of imported goods, it allows domestic producers to raise their prices without fear of competition. This, in fact, was the

---

97. Phil Levy, "Will Trump's Tariffs Have a Silver Lining of Raising Revenue? Don't Bet on It," *Forbes*, April 12, 2018, https://www.forbes.com/sites /phillevy/2018/04/12/trump-tariff-revenue-what-tariff-revenue /#4d449346390f.

98. It is the same reasoning that drives the "Laffer Curve" idea in income taxation—a tax of zero raises no revenue, but a tax that is so high it blocks all activity does not raise any revenue either. That means that at some point revenue falls as the tax increases.

99. You are also limited by the presence of competing domestic firms who are also eager for market share. Note also that in 2017, US domestic steel production accounted for roughly 75 percent of domestic consumption. For more information, see US Department of Commerce, *The Effect of Imports of Steel on the National Security*, January 11, 2018, https://www.bis.doc.gov /index.php/documents/steel/2224-the-effect-of-imports-of-steel-on-the -national-security-with-redactions-20180111/file.

predictable result when the Trump administration imposed widespread tariffs on steel in June 2018.[100] An important implication is that even producers who only bought American-made steel ended up paying for the tariffs through increased prices.

While tariffs have a long tradition and are relatively easy to understand, they have been negotiated down significantly over the decades of the GATT and the WTO. For the United States, in 2017, 100 percent of its tariffs were bound by WTO commitments.[101] Its average tariff was 5.3 percent on agricultural goods and 3.1 percent on nonagricultural goods. Because manufactures and other nonagricultural goods accounted for almost 95 percent of US imports, the simple average MFN-applied tariff for the United States was 3.4 percent.

How does this compare to the rest of the world? Table 1 shows the numbers for some key trading partners, with the United States repeated for easy comparison.[102]

There are several points to note about this. First, agricultural trade is more heavily protected than other types. The United States is a major agricultural exporter, so it has lower tariff protection on that sector. Note, though, that both Canada and Japan have lower average tariffs than the United States outside the agricultural sector.

A second point is that these are MFN tariffs—the amount charged to countries when there is no FTA. The listed Canadian tariffs are not the averages that the United States would pay, for example, since it has (nearly) tariff-free access to the Canadian market through NAFTA.[103] A major purpose of TPP for the United States was to gain tariff-free access to the large Japanese market.

---

100. David Lawder, "U.S. Commerce Dept Probing Steel 'Profiteering' After Tariffs," Reuters, June 20, 2018, https://www.reuters.com/article/us-usa -trade-steel/u-s-commerce-dept-probing-steel-profiteering-after-tariffs -idUSKBN1JG22W.

101. World Trade Organization, "United States of America" (data, Washington, DC: World Trade Organization), https://www.wto.org/english/res_e/statis _e/daily_update_e/tariff_profiles/US_E.pdf.

102. World Trade Organization, "Members and Observers" (data, Washington, DC: World Trade Organization), https://www.wto.org/english/thewto_e /whatis_e/tif_e/org6_e.htm. After clicking on a country, click on "pdf" under "Tariff profile" for MFN tariff rates for that country.

103. Canada has protected agricultural sectors within NAFTA, such as its dairy management system.

Table 1 - Comparison of key trading partners

Country	Agricultural MFN tariff 2017	Nonagricultural MFN tariff 2017	Simple MFN-applied tariff average 2017
Canada	15.7	2.1	4.0
China	15.6	8.8	9.8
European Union	10.8	4.2	5.1
Japan	13.3	2.5	4.0
United States	5.3	3.1	3.4

A third point is that China's tariffs are notably higher than those of the industrialized countries on the list. We would see a similar contrast with other major developing countries, a reflection of the traditional lenience shown to poorer countries when demanding tariff cuts. The table also shows, however, that this developing-country reluctance to cut tariffs comes at a price: many developing countries are important agricultural exporters and have failed to negotiate away agricultural tariffs. That stands in contrast to industrial products, where the developed countries undertook significant liberalization among themselves.

Finally, the table puts discussions about reciprocity in trade into some perspective. It is relatively easy to find specific products where tariffs are unequal across countries (e.g., the United States taxes car imports at 2.5 percent, while the European Union imposes a 10 percent tariff).[104] But the averages show that those asymmetries roughly even out when one looks across a broader range of goods. The United States, for example, imposes a 25 percent tariff on the import of light trucks, the so-called "Chicken Tax," which has lingered from a trade dis-

104. World Trade Organization, "United States and European Auto Tariff Schedule" (data, Washington, DC: World Trade Organization), http://tariffdata.wto.org/ReportersAndProducts.aspx. (The US-EU tariff schedule can be accessed by selecting both the "United States of America" and "European Union" under "Reporters," and by selecting section 8703 under "Products.")

pute in the 1960s when France and Germany put tariffs on the import of US poultry.[105]

What the simple averages conceal is the distribution of tariffs among products. One important analysis of US tariffs in the pre-Trump era showed that most tariff revenue comes from consumer goods and that the impact falls heavily on the poor. Tariffs tend to be high on consumer goods and low on luxury goods.[106]

The ease of analyzing and tallying tariffs makes it tempting to think that tariffs are the *only* trade measure one needs to think about. This sort of thinking is behind the popular idea that a true FTA would fit on a single page.[107] What does it need to do besides declaring all tariffs to be zero?

In fact, as tariffs fell, new forms of protection and new concerns emerged. The most prominent of these are discussed below.

Rules of origin

One important complication to trade rules played a central role in the Trump administration's renegotiation of NAFTA. The major benefit of an FTA like NAFTA is that goods from within the region move freely across borders and are generally not subject to tariffs.

But what is a good from within the region? If a car is made from start to finish in Toledo, Ohio, then it is clearly a North American car. However, this is increasingly rare. Global supply chains mean that sophisticated products are much more commonly made with parts that come from different places around the world.

If we return to our imaginary car and hypothesize that it has parts from the United States, Canada, and Mexico, then it will still clearly be a North American product. But what if it uses some parts from Japan or Germany or Brazil, as many cars do? At what point does it stop being a North American product?

---

105. Nick Fountain, "632: The Chicken Tax," January 25, 2017, in *Planet Money*, produced by Frances Harlow, podcast, MP3 audio, 16:56, https://www.npr .org/templates/transcript/transcript.php?storyId=511663527.

106. Edward Gresser, "Taxing the Poor," *Foreign Affairs*, July 30, 2008, https:// www.foreignaffairs.com/articles/united-states/2008-07-30/taxing-poor.

107. Jonah Goldberg, "Free Speech — Sometimes," *Townhall*, March 1, 2006, https://townhall.com/columnists/jonahgoldberg/2006/03/01/free-speech ---sometimes-n1407826.

This is the question that *rules of origin* set out to answer. There is no clear economic definition. It is a political question, and the answer is negotiated among the member countries. In the original NAFTA, a car made with 62.5 percent North American parts was considered a North American product and not subject to tariffs if shipped within the three member states. In the renegotiated NAFTA, this cutoff was increased to 75 percent, with additional requirements about wages paid to workers in the production of the car.[108]

Rules of origin can have a protectionist effect, tilting purchases toward regional producers and away from the rest of the world. To see how, imagine that, under the old NAFTA, an auto producer figures out the ideal sourcing of parts to minimize costs. Imagine this plan would result in 61.5 percent North American parts. The producer would likely be tempted to substitute some less desirable regional parts for those in the original plan in order to get that percentage up to 62.5 percent and take advantage of the tariff break.[109]

There is a limit, however, to how much additional cost a producer would be willing to incur. In the United States, the MFN tariff on imported autos is 2.5 percent. If the cost of meeting the rules of origin requirement is greater than 2.5 percent, the producer will be better off just giving up on meeting the rules of origin, going with the original sourcing plan, and paying the tariff.[110]

Given how central the new auto rules were to the Trump administration's reworking of NAFTA, suspicions have been raised that the

---

108. Jack Caporal and William Reinsch, "From NAFTA to USMCA: What's New and What's Next?" (Washington, DC: Center for Strategic and International Studies, October 3, 2018), https://www.csis.org/analysis/nafta-usmca-whats -new-and-whats-next.

109. We know the regional parts are less desirable because they were not part of the ideal plan, under our assumptions. This argument was originally made by Krueger and Krishna. See Kala Krishna and Anne Krueger, "Implementing Free Trade Areas: Rules of Origin and Hidden Protection" (working paper, International Trade and Investment, The National Bureau of Economic Research, January 1995), http://www.nber.org/papers/w4983.

110. For a development of this argument, see Caroline Freund, "Streamlining Rules of Origin in NAFTA" (policy brief, Washington, DC: Peterson Institute for International Economics, June 2017), https://piie.com/publications /policy-briefs/streamlining-rules-origin-nafta.

administration will also increase the MFN tariff through a national security action.[111]

An important consideration about rules of origin is the complexity they bring to business management. Companies know where their suppliers are located, but they may not know where their suppliers' suppliers are located. In fact, suppliers are often secretive about such information so as not to get cut out of the process in a cost-saving move. Companies are even less likely to have detailed information about wages paid at their suppliers' suppliers, or even their suppliers. This may mean that imaginative schemes for protecting industries through rules of origin, such as wage-content levels in the revised NAFTA, will prove very difficult to implement and enforce.

Finally, rules of origin are a feature unique to FTAs. They do not apply in a customs union like the European Union. For example, a Chinese exporter selling to the US market might try to sell goods in Canada first and move them across the border later if Canada had a lower tariff than the United States. Rules of origin would prevent that. If the good was not modified in Canada, it would still be considered Chinese when it came into the United States and would be subject to the appropriate tariff.

Customs unions have a common external tariff, so there is no worry about such *trans-shipment*. Goods coming into the United Kingdom, France, Italy, or any other EU country are all subject to the same tariff rate. Once they do, they can move freely across the European Union's internal borders.

That makes life simpler, so long as countries in the customs union can agree on the common tariff. However, if one decides to leave, as the United Kingdom could do under some versions of Brexit, trade gets more complicated again. A major logistical consideration for Britain outside the customs union would be how to meet the rules of origin requirements of an FTA and how to deal with newly imposed tariffs on trade if they do not.

---

111.   Chad Bown, "Sweating the Auto Details of Trump's Trade Deal with Mexico," *Trade & Investment Policy Watch* (blog), Washington, DC: Peterson Institute for International Economics, August 29, 2018, https://piie.com/blogs/trade-investment-policy-watch/sweating-auto-details -trumps-trade-deal-mexico.

Trade balances

Trade deficits have not generally been the subject of trade negotiations—for reasons that will be discussed shortly. But they have taken on a new importance under the Trump administration.

Trade deficits have occupied such a prominent spot in policy debates for two reasons. First, there is a desire for a convenient scorecard. A trade balance *looks* like a scorecard. It seems to show one country up (a surplus—positive!) and one country down (a deficit—negative!). If one draws a comparison to business, it seems analogous to the ideas of sales and market share: the country that sells the most wins. As it happens, that analogy is misguided, but nonetheless tempting.

The second reason has to do with *jobs*. Politicians who want to take credit for trade agreements do not want to make abstract claims about economic efficiency or the reallocation of society's resources. They know voters' eyes will glaze over. Instead, politicians want to talk about how many jobs they have created. But that is not a number that pops out of standard economic analysis.

Because of this, government economists came up with a quick and dirty workaround. They asked how many jobs were linked to exports. Then, they divided the number of jobs by the value of exports. This gave a number of roughly 6,000 jobs per $1 billion of exports.[112] However, the number's significance is dubious. For one, there is a difference between *average* and *marginal* employment. An exporting company that doubles its production does not necessarily have to double employment in its legal or accounting departments. Furthermore, what happens if an economy is at full employment but then shifts production to increase exports? The formula suggests that employment will increase, but capacity constraints say it will not.

No matter—it soon became popular to equate exports with jobs. But if exports meant jobs gained, then, by the same flawed logic, imports meant jobs lost. In turn, that implied that trade surpluses translated to a net job gain while a trade deficit meant a net job loss.

---

112. Chris Rasmussen, *Jobs Supported by Exports 2016: An Update* (Washington, DC: Office of Trade and Economic Analysis, United States Department of Commerce, International Trade Administration, August 2, 2017), https://www.trade.gov/mas/ian/build/groups/public/@tg_ian /documents/webcontent/tg_ian_005543.pdf.

Figure 7 – US trade balance and unemployment rate

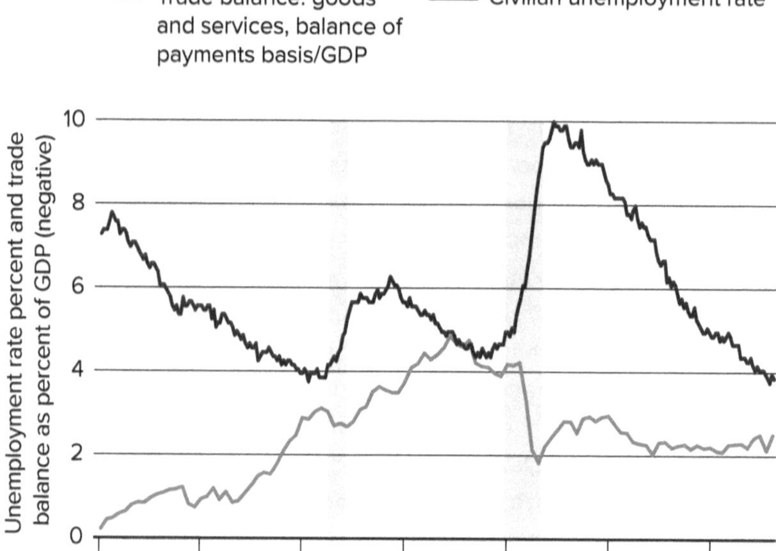

Source: US Bureau of Economic Analysis and US Bureau of the Census, re-trieved from FRED, Federal Reserve Bank of St. Louis, March 18, 2019, https://fred.stlouisfed.org/series/BOPGSTB.

These two ideas—trade balances as a scorecard for policies or per-formance and trade balances as a proxy measure for job creation or loss—are misguided, but wildly popular. To see why they are wrong, one may consider data or theory. Since most people find data more persua-sive, we will begin there.

If trade balances are a good proxy for job gain or loss, they should correlate well with the unemployment rate. All else constant, we should expect to see relatively high unemployment when the trade deficit rises and relatively low unemployment when the trade deficit falls.

If anything, figure 7 shows the opposite for the United States in the last 25 years. In times of recession (shaded in gray), the trade deficit drops, but unemployment increases. Why would this be?

Broader macroeconomic forces affect trade balances and employ-ment. When an economy is booming, consumers have more income and demand more of everything—both goods produced at home and goods produced abroad (imports). If the US economy heats up while other countries' economies idle, imports to the United States will increase while exports hold constant (everything else equal). So a stronger economy will generally correlate with both lower unemployment (workers hired to make more stuff) and a higher trade deficit (imports increasing, exports constant). Empirically, then, there is not much evidence that lower trade deficits correlate with good economic times.

What about the idea that trade balances can serve as a scorecard for successful or unsuccessful trade policy? If, in fact, trade policies determine trade deficits, then two countries with identical trade policies should have identical trade deficits.

To refute this empirically, we turn to Europe to compare Germany and France.[113] They are the two largest economies in Europe, are geographically adjacent, and have *identical* trade policies. This last point is because the European Union negotiates trade policy as a single bloc. There are no French tariffs or German tariffs, only EU tariffs.

Yet over a period of decades, identical trade policies produced very different trade balances. In recent years, Germany had a large surplus (as a share of GDP) and France a deficit.

The explanation is the same as above: trade balances are driven by macroeconomic forces and are not really the result of trade policies. Germany and France differed in their levels of saving and investment. If that last explanation sounded like a *non sequitur*, it may be time for a little theory.

So far, we have used the term "trade balance" loosely, as the difference between exports and imports. Now, we can specify that the trade balance refers to trade in goods and services. There are two other common variants: the *current account balance* and the *merchandise trade balance*. The current account balance is the broadest of the three, also incorporating payments on investments owned abroad.[114] The merchandise trade balance is the narrowest, as it excludes trade in services. It is also the most reported, so it grabs more than its share of headlines.

113. Phil Levy, "The German Art of the Deal," *Forbes*, March 18, 2017, https://www.forbes.com/sites/phillevy/2017/03/18/the-german-art-of-the -deal/#492388c3225f.

114. Greg Mankiw, "The Current Account vs the Trade Deficit," *Random Observations for Students of Economics* (blog), July 1, 2006, https://gregmankiw.blogspot.com/2006/07/current-acccount-vs-trade -deficit.html.

Figure 8 – Trade balances of Germany and France, 1980–2016

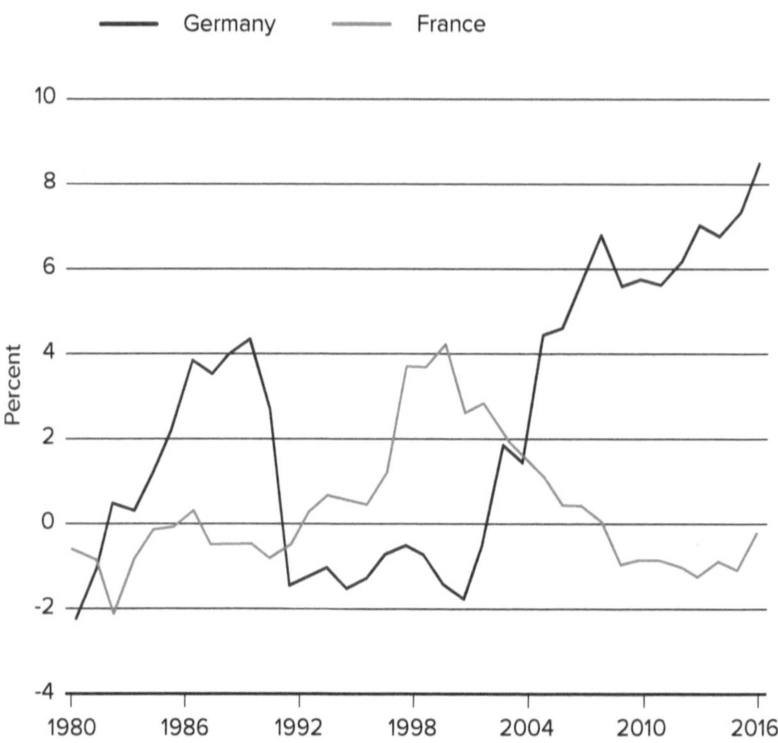

Source: The World Bank, "Current Account Balance (% of GDP)" (data on Germany and France, Geneva: The World Bank), https://data.worldbank.org/indicator/BN.CAB.XOKA.GD.ZS?end=2017&locations=DE-FR&start=1971&view=chart.

The United States is particularly good at producing services and runs a services trade surplus. This means that there are very different descriptions of US trade balances with the same country. In 2017 the United States ran a $376 billion merchandise trade deficit with China, but only a $335 billion overall trade deficit. The difference was due to a $40 billion services trade surplus.[115]

Where do investment and savings policies come in? To see this, we need to look at all the transactions that take place between countries.

---

115. "The People's Republic of China," Office of the United States Trade Representative, https://ustr.gov/countries-regions/china-mongolia-taiwan/peoples-republic-china.

This is known as *balance of payments* accounting.[116] Rather than delve into the details, here's a simple example in which the world has only two countries: the United States and China.

Let's suppose that the United States wants to borrow money from China. It does so by selling a bond to Chinese investors. Here we encounter a problem. In this example, Chinese citizens and investors spend renminbi (RMB), the Chinese national currency. But US citizens spend dollars. So now, after our imaginary bond sale, US investors are left holding, let's say, 10 billion RMB.

What does one do with 10 billion RMB? Perhaps the instinctual answer is to take it to the currency exchange and swap it for dollars. But that merely passes the problem off to the person with whom the currency was swapped. Ultimately, those 10 billion RMB have to find their way back to China. Consider two possibilities.

In the first scenario, the 10 billion RMB are used to buy a Chinese bond. In this case, China lent 10 billion RMB to the United States, and the United States lent it right back to China. This would all be tallied in the "financial account" for balance of payments purposes and would show up as zero net lending.

In the second scenario, the 10 billion RMB are used to buy Chinese steel, mobile phones, and microwaves. In this case, the United States would run a surplus on the "financial account"—exporting financial instruments, such as the services required for transacting in RMB—and a deficit on the "current account"—importing more than it exports.[117]

What do we take from this example? Trade balances are the flip side of borrowing and lending. That is not an abstract theory. It is accounting—just keeping tabs on money flows. This takes no stance on whether borrowing causes trade deficits or trade deficits cause borrowing. It just argues that the two go together. It explains why economists will argue that a large increase in public borrowing (as in the federal budget deficit) will increase the trade deficit unless it is offset by an increase in private savings.

The other lesson is that these are transactions that take place over time. In both our simple example and in recent real life, the United States ended up with a pile of goods and services, while China ended

---

116. "Balance of Payments," Federal Reserve Bank of New York, https://www.newyorkfed.org/aboutthefed/fedpoint/fed40.html.
117. Another way to think about this is that the United States is really borrowing goods and services from China, not RMB.

up with a pile of IOUs. That's a little poetic license—China actually ended up with dollar-denominated Treasury bonds, or bank accounts, or real estate holdings. But it cannot eat or wear or drive any of those things. The only thing it can do with them is buy dollar-denominated goods and services at some point in the future.

In our simple example, the world had only two countries. What if there are really more than that? Actually, there are currently 164 members of the WTO. Does that change the trade deficit story?[118]

It does in a couple of important ways. First, we now have two types of trade deficit numbers: overall trade balances (e.g., the difference between total US exports and total US imports) and bilateral trade balances (e.g., the difference between US exports to and imports from China or any other country). The first, broader balance corresponds with the borrowing and lending story above. The bilateral deficits are economically meaningless, but they have a strong grip on both the public imagination and current trade policy discussions.

To see why bilateral deficits are economically meaningless, let's expand our hypothetical world above to include three "countries": the United States, China, and the Middle East. Suppose China exports $100 billion of manufactures to the United States, the United States exports $100 billion of wheat to the Middle East, and the Middle East exports $100 billion of oil to China. This is sometimes referred to as "triangular trade"—something more sophisticated than simple swaps between countries.

In this example, each country runs a $100 billion bilateral trade deficit with one country and a $100 billion bilateral trade surplus with the other. But each country has perfectly balanced trade overall. Even if we wanted to pass judgment on borrowing and lending, there would be nothing to judge. Of course, there can be bilateral imbalances along with multilateral imbalances, but the economic import comes only from the broader measures.

The misleading nature of bilateral trade balances becomes even more apparent when we consider global supply chains. Returning to the real world with many different countries and products, suppose the United States imports $100 billion of a product that is finished in Malaysia. Then, as China emerges onto the trading scene,

---

118. "Members and Observers," World Trade Organization, https://www.wto.org/english/thewto_e/whatis_e/tif_e/org6_e.htm.

Box 2 – Trade deficits and the economy

> It's Econ 101 that GDP equals the sum of domestic economic activity plus 'net exports,' i.e., exports minus imports. Therefore, when we run massive and chronic trade deficits, it weakens our economy.
>
> —Peter Navarro, PhD

Actually, that is a common misreading of Economics 101. The familiar breakdown of economic activity is given by the formula:

$Y = C + I + G + (X - M)$ where Y is GDP, C is consumption, I is investment, and G is government spending. The last term is exports minus imports, or the trade balance.

Other things being equal, a decrease in $X - M$ would drive down GDP. Does this not show that trade deficits shrink the economy?

No, because other things are not equal. To see this, think of an American consumer who decides to purchase a $30,000 car made in Germany. This enters into the above equation as an increase in C (consumption) and as an increase in M (an import). Those two changes would cancel out, which is exactly what we would want, given that Y is supposed to measure domestic production and the car was made in Europe.

The point of subtracting imports is to avoid double counting spending on private consumption, investment goods, or government purchases that did not originate at home. Note the flip side: taxing foreign cars to the point where our consumer forgoes the imported Volkswagen cuts both C and M and does nothing to lift Y.

the final stage of production of this good shifts from Kuala Lumpur to Guangzhou. Now, $90 billion worth of production is done in Malaysia and $10 billion is done in China, after which the completed good is shipped to the United States. What does this do to bilateral trade balances?

The way exports are measured by the WTO does not count the value added. It only counts final sales. Therefore, this switch would decrease Malaysia's measured exports to the United States by $100 billion and increase China's measured exports by $100 billion, even though the actual switch was only of $10 billion of production.[119]

This problem is pervasive in a world of global supply chains, where parts and partially completed products zip back and forth across borders all the time. By one estimate, if the US trade deficit with China were measured in value-added terms in 2014, it would have been reduced 35 percent from the reported value.[120]

What does all this imply about trade policy? There may be a reason to worry about overall trade deficits, but only because they can reflect international borrowing. Borrowing, of course, may be good or bad, depending on what the borrowed funds are used for. The numbers *cannot* be interpreted as a measure of trade policy-induced losses, a drag on GDP, or a killer of jobs.

What if the United States demands that other countries "fix" a bilateral trade deficit? First, they may respond with a lesson in macroeconomics, as South Korea initially tried when Trump attacked the US–Korea FTA (KORUS).[121] Second, they may argue that there is no bilateral trade deficit when one properly accounts for services, as Canada did in NAFTA talks.[122] Third, they may offer baubles—some extra purchases redirected from other countries, as China attempted.[123]

But there is no trade policy lever to "fix" a trade deficit, and it would not do much to boost US well-being if there were. It is difficult to adopt the right trade policy while pursuing the wrong objective.

---

119. This example deliberately corresponds with some contemporary estimates of Chinese trading in the early 2000s, which put Chinese value added at around 10 percent.

120. David Hoffman and Erik Lundh, "'Huge' Trade Deficits Are Smaller Than You Think," *Bloomberg*, March 18, 2018, https://www.bloomberg.com/view /articles/2018-03-18/big-u-s-china-trade-deficit-is-smaller-than-it-appears.

121. "S. Korean Negotiator Vows to Put National Interest First in U.S. Trade Talks," Yonhap News Agency, January 5, 2018, http://english.yonhapnews .co.kr/business/2018/01/05/0502000000AEN20180105000300315.html.

122. "Trump Says He Made Up Facts About Trade Deficit in Meeting with Trudeau," CBC, March 15, 2018, https://www.cbc.ca/news/politics/trump -trudeau-1.4577179.

123. "China's Reported Offer to Slash Trade Deficit with US Is About Politics: Economist," CNBC, May 18, 2018, https://www.cnbc.com/2018/05/18/us -china-trade-chinas-offer-is-more-politics-than-economics.html.

Currency manipulation

In his 2011 book *Death by China*, Peter Navarro wrote, "If money is the root of all evil, then China's manipulation of its currency, the yuan, is the tap root of everything wrong with the U.S.–China trade relationship. . . . [It] is threatening to tear asunder the entire global economic fabric and free trade framework."[124]

It is not hard to see why there is a push to include controls on currency in trade agreements. Suppose an American firm produces a product to sell in China for $100. Initially, let's assume an exchange rate of 6.5 RMB to the dollar and a Chinese tariff of 10 percent. That $100 American product becomes $110 after the tariff and 715 RMB after currency conversion. Let's assume there is a Chinese-produced competitive product selling for 700 RMB. The American company then has a difficult time selling its exports.

Suppose that China is somehow persuaded to drop its 10 percent tariff. That alone should mean that the American product will now sell for 650 RMB ($100 x 6.5), which should put it in a strong position against the competing Chinese firm.

But if the RMB were to depreciate[125] to 7.15 RMB to the dollar, the American product would once again be priced at 715 RMB in China, despite the removal of the tariff.

Does this not show that currency manipulation can serve to tilt the playing field in a way that offsets trade liberalization? In fact, such allegations were specifically made against China—that it was distorting its currency to the benefit of domestic Chinese producers.[126]

It is the case that currency movements affect the relative price competitiveness of traded goods. The next section will consider the question of whether this ought to be a forbidden subsidy. In this section, we

---

124. Isaac Stone Fish, "Trump's China-Bashing Id," *Slate*, December 22, 2016, https://slate.com/news-and-politics/2016/12/peter-navarro-trumps-trade-czar-embodies-the-china-bashing-id-of-his-campaign.html.

125. One confusing aspect of discussing currencies is why a move from 6.5 to 7.15 would be considered a *depreciation* (downward move) in the Chinese currency. Didn't the numbers go up? A way to think about this is how much do Chinese have to pay for dollars? The more they have to pay, the weaker their currency relative to the dollar.

126. While the example given concerned an American firm trying to sell into China, the same effect would occur for a Chinese firm selling into the United States (i.e., a depreciated RMB would result in lower US prices for the Chinese product).

Figure 9 – USD–EUR exchange rate

Source: Board of Governors of the Federal Reserve System (US), retrieved from FRED, Federal Reserve Bank of St. Louis, February 13, 2019, https://fred.stlouisfed.org/series/DEXUSEU.

look at the more general questions of what drives currency movements, some recent experience with those movements in the Chinese context, and how one might think about illicit currency manipulation.

If we were to consider whether the example above, in which the RMB depreciated from 6.5 to 7.15, was an objectionable act by the Chinese government, the first question to ask is why the currency depreciated.

There are three broad categories of exchange rate regimes to consider: *floating*, *fixed*, and *managed float*.

Floating marks one extreme, in which exchange rates are set purely by market forces. This is a good description of how the US dollar moves against the euro. Each day currency traders place bids to buy or sell one currency for the other.[127] Neither the US government nor any major Eurozone entity is targeting an exchange rate. As figure 9 shows, this results in substantial exchange rate movements, with more than 30 percent movement in the value of the dollar from peak to trough.[128]

No one would really describe this as currency manipulation, though the movements have the same relative effects on the price of goods that we described in the Chinese example. Interestingly, these movements cannot be excused on the grounds that governments played no role. Governments *did* play a role. It was just an indirect one. As a general rule, tighter monetary policy is associated with higher interest rates and will drive up the relative value of a currency. Looser monetary policy will do the reverse. Both the Federal Reserve System in the United States and the European Central Bank were actively conducting monetary policy during the time period in figure 9.

But the changes they made in interest rates and in their balance sheets were not primarily targeted at exchange rates. They certainly influenced the exchange rate, but they were more directed at sustaining domestic growth, maintaining full employment, and keeping prices stable (warding off inflation or deflation).

If we return to the example of the Chinese RMB against the dollar, we can see examples of both a *fixed exchange rate* and a *managed float*.

In the period leading up to mid-2005, the RMB was fixed at 8.28 to the dollar (see figure 10). This may seem like an extreme version of currency intervention, but it was the kind of policy that was considered a best practice for decades after World War II. Countries might adopt fixed exchange rate regimes to assure people that they would not indulge in printing money, for example. This could work because a fixed exchange rate requires countries to tighten or loosen monetary policy

---

127. Foreign currency markets have enormous volume. Daily trading volumes can average well over $1.5 *trillion*.

128. In this graph, high numbers indicate a weak dollar and a strong euro. Low numbers indicate a strong dollar and a weak euro.

Figure 10 – USD–RMB exchange rate

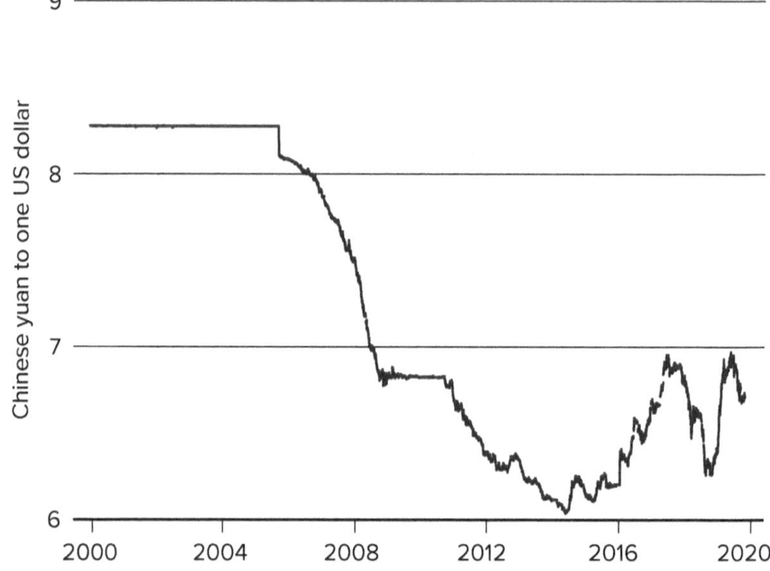

Source: Board of Governors of the Federal Reserve System (US), retrieved from FRED, Federal Reserve Bank of St. Louis, February 13, 2019, https://fred. stlouisfed.org/series/DEXCHUS.

as demanded by currency traders, not according to a central bank's discretion.[129]

China tried to defend its exchange rate this way. As more money tried to come into than out of China in the early 2000s, China accumulated foreign exchange reserves (see figure 11). Countries are supposed to have foreign exchange reserves, so there was nothing wrong with this per se. But it started to get out of hand. The United States pushed strongly for China to appreciate the RMB, particularly since China's bilateral trade surplus with the United States had ballooned before its overall trade surplus did.

---

129. There is a twist on this if one allows for capital controls. The interaction between fixed exchange rates, independent monetary policy, and capital controls is known as the "impossible trinity." This is beyond the scope of our discussion here. For further reading on this topic, see "What Is the Impossible Trinity?" *The Economist*, September 10, 2016, https://www .economist.com/the-economist-explains/2016/09/09/what-is-the -impossible-trinity.

Figure 11 – Foreign exchange reserves of China

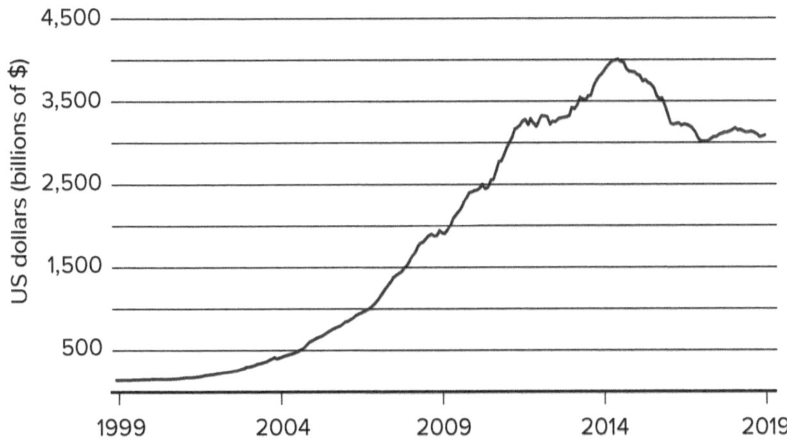

Source: International Monetary Fund, retrieved from FRED, Federal Reserve Bank of St. Louis, March 18, 2019, https://fred.stlouisfed.org/series /TRESEGCNM052N.

As China showed increasing prowess as an exporter, critics charged it with currency manipulation.[130] After all, the currency was initially fixed and therefore not determined by market forces. Accumulating foreign exchange reserves could be taken as evidence of pressure to appreciate.

So what was China to do? It could hold its currency fixed, it could allow it to float freely, or it could do something in between—a *managed float*. China went for the last option. It set reference bands each day and allowed the currency to move within those bands. That meant that if the currency moved too far, the People's Bank of China would intervene. The result was that the RMB appreciated 6 to 8 percent per year from roughly 2005 to 2014, excluding a pause in response to the global financial crisis.

Was this currency manipulation? Was China trying to gain a commercial advantage? Or was it simply engaging in ordinary management of the economy? Consider the alternatives China faced. From the perspec-

---

130. Notably, the Department of the Treasury repeatedly opted not to charge China with currency manipulation, and it is the official arbiter for the United States.

tive of its critics, keeping the fixed exchange rate was the worst thing it could do. Would a float have been better? Actually, the US government did not press China to float its currency. There was—and remains—concern that if China did that, the currency might actually depreciate, making Chinese exports even more competitive.

If we eliminate those two extremes, we are left with some sort of managed appreciation of the currency, which is exactly what China pursued.[131] Critics could have argued that the appreciation was not fast enough, but there was a serious concern that double-digit currency appreciation could have badly damaged the Chinese economy and, in turn, the global economy. After all, China had many small businesses that had operated under a fixed exchange rate for years.

During this period, the United States had a process, run by the Department of the Treasury, to assess whether countries were manipulating their currency. Both Obama and Trump vowed to find China to be a currency manipulator, if elected. Both were elected, and neither did. The law (changed over time) that gives guidance on what constitutes currency manipulation[132] stipulates that three criteria must be met for a country to be labeled a currency manipulator. The Department of the Treasury cited three criteria in the spring of 2018:

1. A bilateral trade surplus of at least $20 billion with the United States,

2. A current account surplus of at least 3 percent of GDP, and

3. Persistent, one-sided intervention in currency markets of sufficient magnitude.

The first criterion makes no economic sense, but the other two do. China's current account surplus peaked at over 10 percent of GDP in 2007, but fell below the 3 percent threshold by 2011 and was 1.4 percent of GDP in 2017.[133] Furthermore, in recent years, China actually spent down reserves in an effort to bolster the value of its currency. In its most re-

---

131. *China's Exchange Rate Policy* (statement by Philip I. Levy).

132. United States Department of the Treasury, *Macroeconomic and Foreign Exchange Policies of Major Trading Partners of the United States* (Washington, DC: Office of International Affairs, United States Department of the Treasury, October 2018), https://home.treasury.gov/system/files/206/2018-10-17-%28Fall-2018-FX%20Report%29.pdf.

133. United States Department of the Treasury, *Macroeconomic and Foreign Exchange Policies*, 17.

cent 2018 report, the Department of the Treasury found that no country qualified as a currency manipulator.

There are two fundamental problems with introducing currency manipulation into the trade debate, a conceptual one and a practical one. The conceptual problem is that monetary policies move currencies and are an accepted part of macroeconomic management. When the US economy faltered in the fall of 2008, the Federal Reserve undertook extraordinary monetary policies to try to revive it. Other things being equal, those policy decisions would be expected to have an effect on the value of the dollar, though that was not the primary target of the Federal Reserve's efforts. The point is that it is very difficult to distinguish between standard, acceptable monetary policy and currency manipulation.

The practical difficulty is that monetary policy is generally separate from trade policy. In the United States, Congress and various departments of the executive branch set trade policy. Monetary policy is set by the Federal Reserve, which is independent. This central bank independence is considered an essential part of good economic governance. It is difficult, if not impossible, to put binding restrictions on exchange rate policy in trade agreements without damaging central bank independence.

Subsidies and state-owned enterprises

The problem of currency manipulation discussed in the previous section is emblematic of a broader class of trade complaints. These occur when trade and competition are seen as unfair, such as when a government takes actions that could either advantage or disadvantage businesses competing across borders. In this section, we will look at the broader question of subsidies and, relatedly, state-owned enterprises.

It is not hard to define a government subsidy. It occurs when a government takes an action to allow a good to be sold for a lower price. The hard part is defining an objectionable subsidy.

Consider a whole range of actions that we would probably not want to include as objectionable subsidies:

▶ **Public education.** When the government educates future workers, they are more productive. That drives down the cost of producing goods.

- ▶ **Infrastructure.** When the government provides high-quality roads or ports, it makes it less costly to move goods around and thus lowers the price.

- ▶ **Support for the financial sector.** By offering services such as deposit insurance, a government bolsters the banking sector which, in turn, lowers the cost of borrowing for producers.

- ▶ **Defense and domestic security.** By incurring these costs, the government relieves businesses from having to undertake their own security expenditures, thereby lowering prices.

The above list is hardly exhaustive, but it is meant to illustrate the various ways in which a government can lower costs for businesses. Since governments engage in these activities to different degrees, these advantages are unlikely to be enjoyed equally across countries. Hence, they are affecting outcomes of international competition. But we generally do not think of them as unfair.

Members of the global trading system have grappled with this issue and come up with some ways of distinguishing those subsidies they *do* consider unfair.

The most basic prohibited subsidy, dating back to the beginning of the GATT, is an export subsidy, or any kind of payment from the government that is directly tied to export performance.[134] This prohibition was applied to industrial products, but the regime governing agricultural products has been much more permissive. This illustrates one of the key themes of subsidies governance: unfair subsidies are the ones *your* government does not want to use. There was no consensus to ban export subsidies in agriculture as there had been for manufactures. Hence, agricultural subsidies went largely unscathed.

Beyond blocking export subsidies for manufactures, the GATT offered two other key concepts for distinguishing fair from unfair: problematic subsidies were specific and involved a financial contribution.[135] Specificity meant that the subsidy was intended to help a particular company, industry, or region. This would rule out the government pro-

---

134. "Export Competition/Subsidies," World Trade Organization, https://www.wto.org/english/tratop_e/agric_e/ag_intro04_export_e.htm.

135. "Agreement on Subsidies and Countervailing Measures ('SCM Agreement')," World Trade Organization, https://www.wto.org/english /tratop_e/scm_e/subs_e.htm.

Box 3 - The debate over subsidies in the airline industry

One of the most contentious global fights over subsidies took place in its own separate category—large, civil aircraft. In reality, that meant Boeing versus Airbus.

The economics of the aircraft industry require large up-front investments in development and production. One implication is that there is no room in the global market for lots of small, competitive producers. Instead, a small number of very large producers compete to potentially grab a large pot of profits. And their governments may want to help them capture that pot.

The United States accused Europe of subsidizing Airbus, while Europe accused the United States of subsidizing Boeing. More specifically, the United States alleged that the European Union provided "launch aid," or money to cover the large up-front costs associated with producing an Airbus passenger jet line. The European Union, in turn, argued that the state of Washington had subsidized Boeing by providing tax breaks. Further, it said that the United States had effectively provided its own launch aid for Boeing by buying similar military aircraft at cost. (In the presence of "learning by doing," the first planes will normally be more expensive than later planes to produce. If so, it helps if that cost does not need to be spread over the entire production run.)

viding education, financial regulation, or public security, for example, as those are available to all businesses and industries.

Financial contribution generally meant that money had to pass from the government to the specific recipient. It could be through a grant, subsidized loan, or purchasing guarantee, for example, but it had to be money going to the company. This ruled out examples such as the provision of roads and ports that were generally available.

Even if the concept of subsidies is narrowed in this way, it still calls into question some popular US programs in recent years such as the use of public funds to keep Chrysler and General Motors alive in the wake of the global financial crisis. That was government money directed for the specific benefit of two auto manufacturers.

Despite the difficulty of defining which subsidies are objectionable, countries have the right under WTO rules to respond to subsidies, provided they follow the right procedures. This is commonly referred to as "countervailing duties" (CVDs)—tariffs applied to counteract subsidies applied to another country's exports. The United States has had such a program in place since 1930.[136]

The details of the procedure are complex, but the basic idea is that a company or industry competing against imports to the United States that it considers unfair must show that (1) those imports have been subsidized and (2) those subsidies caused injury. In the United States, the first investigation is carried out by the Department of Commerce, and the second by the USITC.[137] The Department of Commerce determines the extent of any subsidy. The USITC determines whether the subsidy injured US industry. The CVD response is a major source of US tariffs against other countries.

One celebrated recent action concerned Canadian softwood lumber.[138] The United States claimed that Canada underpriced access to public lands for logging, effectively providing a subsidy. As a result of the investigation, the United States imposed tariffs exceeding 20 percent on imports from Canada, imports that exceeded $5 billion in value in 2016. One estimate found that the imposition of the CVD raised the average price of a single-family home in the United States by $9,000.[139]

An important variant of the subsidy question concerns state-owned enterprises (SOEs). If the government and a business are completely separate entities, one might expect to observe instances when the business receives financial contributions from the government.

But what happens if the government owns the business? First, any subsidy may be harder to observe. For example, the government might compensate the CEO by promoting that person to a more desirable

---

136. "Understanding Antidumping & Countervailing Duty Investigations," United States International Trade Commission, https://www.usitc.gov/press_room/usad.htm.

137. Each investigation may produce a preliminary and final finding, potentially meaning four announcements per case. Note: there is no White House review stage in the CVD process.

138. "US Sets Final Tariffs on Softwood Lumber from Canada," BBC, November 2, 2017, https://www.bbc.com/news/world-us-canada-41838828.

139. Caroline Basile, "NAHB: Lumber Tariffs Increasing Cost of Homebuilding," *Housingwire*, June 14, 2018, https://www.housingwire.com/articles/43690-nahb-lumber-tariffs-increasing-cost-of-homebuilding.

post rather than with a transfer of cash. Likewise, an SOE might be able to take greater risks than a private enterprise since it need not worry about accountability to shareholders or its stock price.

Beyond these concerns, there is a broader worry that SOEs may not be motivated by economic profit and loss, but could be trying to meet the political objectives of their home governments. One common concern expressed about Chinese SOEs investing in the United States is that they might become large employers in a key congressional district, then wield their influence to sway votes on legislation (e.g., by threatening to close the plant).

Although SOEs are not unique to China, Chinese SOEs are easily the source of concern in the United States. At the time of China's accession to the WTO,[140] it seemed as though China was on course to seriously reduce or even eliminate its massive SOE sector.[141] Subsequently, Chinese President Xi Jinping has made clear that he expects SOEs to play a "leading role" in the future Chinese economy.[142]

The situation becomes even more complicated when relationships between enterprises and governments do not involve 100 percent government ownership. Is there a threshold of ownership below which the company can be considered a private enterprise? What if there is a company such as Huawei, for example, which is not owned by the Chinese government, but which US authorities have warned is heavily influenced by it?[143]

Subsidies are central to public allegations of unfairness, but the point at which subsidies become unfair is difficult to define. Often, the accusations presume that any government financial intervention is unfair and therefore must be prohibited by an organization such as the WTO.

---

140. Phil Levy, "Was Letting China into the WTO a Mistake?" *Foreign Affairs*, April 2, 2018, https://www.foreignaffairs.com/articles/china/2018-04-02 /was-letting-china-wto-mistake?cid=int-fls&pgtype=hpg.

141. Phil Levy, "The Treatment of Chinese SOEs in China's WTO Protocol of Accession" (working paper RSCAS 2017/04, Robert Schuman Centre for Advanced Studies, European University Institute), http://cadmus.eui.eu /bitstream/handle/1814/45984/RSCAS_2017_04.pdf?sequence=1 &isAllowed=y.

142. Arthur Krober, "Xi Jinping's Ambitious Agenda for Economic Reform in China," The Brookings Institute, November 17, 2013, https://www.brookings .edu/opinions/xi-jinpings-ambitious-agenda-for-economic-reform-in-china.

143. Natasha Bach, "Don't Use Huawei Phones, Warn 6 Top U.S. Intelligence Chiefs," *Fortune*, February 14, 2018, http://fortune.com/2018/02/14 /intelligence-chiefs-warn-against-using-huawei-phones.

There are, however, ample practices that critics may consider unfair but are not yet prohibited. Extending such prohibitions would be the task of a future trade agreement, though reaching a strong agreement would be very difficult politically. The problem is that countries' "offensive" demands—the practices they would like to prohibit—are tempered by their "defensive" concerns—their own practices they would like to protect.

Antidumping and safeguards

The companion policy to CVDs is known as antidumping (AD) policy.[144] The pairing is so common that trade mavens will often refer to "AD/CVD" as a type of protection. The two programs are similar in that, if applied properly, they allow protection without a new act of Congress and require separate determinations of injury (by the USITC) and the magnitude of the misdeed (by the Department of Commerce).[145] They are both based on allegations of unfair practices, and together they account for the bulk of barriers to trade in the interval between tariff liberalization under trade agreements and the more aggressive policies of the Trump administration.

AD is distinct from CVD in that the transgression it addresses is selling goods and services at "less than fair value." This can be determined in two principal ways: (1) when an exporting company sells at a lower price in its target market than it does in a reference market (usually the country of origin) or (2) when a company is selling below cost. In each case the gap between the "fair" price and the actual price is referred to as the dumping margin. The result of an affirmative investigation will be the imposition of tariffs to raise the price of the imported good by the amount of the dumping margin.

Why it is unfair for a company to offer a low price? As consumers, the more common complaint is being overcharged, not undercharged. The most plausible economic reason is that a company is trying to drive a competitor out of business (a practice known as "predatory pricing"). The idea is that the short-term loss on below-cost sales will be compensated by higher monopoly prices once competitors are gone.

---

144. For an authoritative discussion of antidumping policy, see Bruce A. Blonigen and Thomas J. Prusa, "Dumping and Antidumping Duties" (working paper 21573, NBER, 2015).
145. "Understanding Antidumping & Countervailing Duty Investigations," United States International Trade Commission.

Domestically, there are procedures for questioning such practices, generally under the rubric of antitrust or competition policies. Yet in practice, antidumping policies do not ask such questions and simply look for price differences.

Such differences are substantially easier to find when the exporting country is considered a nonmarket economy. In such cases, there is a presumption that reported costs are unreliable and that costs can be constructed only with data from third countries. This results in systematically larger antidumping margins. It is why China is so eager to attain market economy status—something it believes it was promised when it joined the WTO.[146]

Antidumping also makes headlines as an example of the United States losing WTO disputes. This has been especially notable in the WTO's rejection of dubious US practices in setting dumping margins. The prime example is "zeroing."[147] To understand the issue, imagine that for the first six months of every year a company sells a good for $10 less in the United States than in Japan. For the other six months, it sells the good for $10 more in the United States than in Japan. Thus, on average, the company sells the same good for the same price in the two countries ($\frac{1}{2} \times 10 + \frac{1}{2} \times (-10)$). Under zeroing, the Department of Commerce would "zero" out the months in which there was a higher price in the United States on the grounds that no dumping occurred then. Thus, the average dumping margin would be $5 ($\frac{1}{2} \times 10 + \frac{1}{2} \times 0$). The United States has repeatedly lost WTO cases on this practice, only to tweak the practice and be challenged again.

Whereas AD and CVD policies are seen as remedies to addressing unfair trade practices, "safeguards" provide similar protection without allegations of unfairness. Safeguards provide breathing room for an industry to respond to a surge in import competition. One rationale is

---

146. The relevant section of the Protocol of Accession, 15(a), said China could be treated as a nonmarket economy for 15 years. Given a start date of December 2001, China interpreted this as meaning that as of December 2016, China would be treated as a market economy. Europe and the United States said it meant that after 15 years, China would have to pass a market economy test—and that China does not currently meet that test. China has contested this at the WTO. See "China Takes on the EU at the WTO," *The Economist*, December 7, 2017, https://www.economist.com /finance-and-economics/2017/12/07/china-takes-on-the-eu-at-the-wto.

147. "What Is Zeroing?" (press release, European Commission, February 6, 2012), http://europa.eu/rapid/press-release_MEMO-12-73_en.htm.

that the existence of such an insurance policy may allow policymakers to lower trade barriers more confidently, knowing that they have a recourse if things turn out worse than expected.

As with AD/CVD, safeguards require a USITC investigation to determine injury and are within WTO rules if applied correctly.[148] Not only is there no allegation of unfairness, but there is also discretion on the part of the president. If it finds injury, the USITC makes a recommendation to the president on what remedy might be applied.

White House discretion was a major reason why safeguard cases had become infrequent in recent decades. Presidents often decided that such protection would not be in the national interest. One important exception occurred in March 2002 when President Bush decided to impose protection on steel imports using a safeguard procedure. The safeguard was ultimately removed after the WTO ruled it had been applied incorrectly.[149]
A review of multiple studies of the episode later concluded that the aggregate costs of the measure exceeded the benefits for the economy in terms of both production and employment.[150] Of course, the action also failed to deliver a healthy and independent steel industry: steel remained dependent on protection, predominantly through AD/CVD measures, and ultimately received additional protection from the Trump administration (though not as a safeguard).

Trump revived the use of safeguards, among other instruments, when he approved safeguard protection for solar panels and washing machines in January 2018.[151]

---

148. "Understanding Safeguard Investigations," United States International Trade Commission, https://www.usitc.gov/press_room/us_safeguard.htm.

149. "United States – Definitive Safeguard Measures of Imports of Certain Steel Products," World Trade Organization, https://www.wto.org/english /tratop_e/dispu_e/cases_e/ds252_e.htm.

150. Robert Read, "The Political Economy of Trade Protection: The Determinants and Welfare Impact of the 2002 US Emergency Steel Safeguard Measures," *World Economy* 28, no. 8 (2005): 1119–37.

151. United States Trade Representative, "President Trump Approves Relief for U.S. Washing Machine and Solar Cell Manufacturers" (press release, Washington, DC: Office of the United States Trade Representative, January 22, 2018), https://ustr.gov/about-us/policy-offices/press-office /press-releases/2018/january/president-trump-approves-relief-us.

Investment and investor-state dispute settlement

One common critique of modern trade agreements is that they extend well beyond trade into the realm of investment and investor protection. In some ways, this is a natural by-product of the evolving nature of international trade. In the 19th century, David Ricardo described a world in which one country made wine, another made cloth, and their tall sailing ships laden with each would pass each other out at sea. In modern trade, it is exceedingly common for the exporting firm in one country and the importing business in another to be linked as parent and affiliate. Particularly when considering international delivery of services, it can be important to have offices in the country where the services are to be delivered. Thus, trade and investment are increasingly linked.

When firms invest capital abroad, either through the acquisition of a domestic firm or by directly building production facilities, it is considered *foreign direct investment* (FDI). Since the end of World War II, FDI has grown and become central to today's globally integrated economies and supply chains.

Investment rules have never had quite the same standing as trade rules in the global system. In the Uruguay Round of trade talks, action was taken against distortions linked to investment such as the requirement that any potential investor agree to purchase a certain amount of local content rather than import materials. Such policies were grouped under the Agreement on Trade-Related Investment Measures. While the WTO has some prohibitions on such behavior, a broader attempt to finalize a Multilateral Agreement on Investment failed.

Beyond the possibility of distortions, a firm that makes an investment abroad is substantially more exposed to risk than one that simply ships a product off in a crate. For firms to feel comfortable that these far-flung investments are safe—being made outside the jurisdiction of their home country—there has been pressure for additional safeguards to be built into trade agreements to protect against expropriation.

This tool, known as the investor-state dispute settlement (ISDS) mechanism, has been a staple of US FTAs for decades. If it simply forbade the seizure of foreign-owned factories, there would be little controversy. For an investor, however, it can be equally worrying if a foreign government acts capriciously to render an investment worthless.

This could happen, for example, if a key input of production was suddenly banned.

This puts investment regulation in the same position as other regulatory issues in trade—trying to differentiate between serious regulatory efforts to protect the public welfare and invidious attempts to block trade or extort payments from a defenseless investor. The ISDS arbitration mechanism was intended to distinguish between these two possibilities. It was to offer relief in the latter case and allow regulation in the former.

There are three main concerns regarding the ISDS mechanism. The first is that it invalidates and supersedes domestic laws and sovereignty. Second, the process for appointing arbitrators is seen as undemocratic. Finally, the lack of transparency in the decision-making process and the closed nature of ISDS cases is unpopular. Let's take each of these in turn.

One of the larger criticisms of the ISDS mechanism is that it circumvents the courts and legal structure of a sovereign state. Although few would defend the actions of autocratic regimes nationalizing entire industries, the use of ISDS in policy arenas often regarded as domestic, such as environmental regulation or consumer safety, is often seen as going against the will of the electorate. Such worries helped motivate European protests over TTIP because of concerns about arbitration panels subverting European law, for example.

The second main complaint is that the process for selecting judges and arbiters is by appointment. Because the investment courts hold such power and tribunals are often staffed with those familiar with the corporate entities involved, these judicial bodies are viewed skeptically by many civil society groups who argue they have too much authority over the fate of consumers.

Finally, the cases are also closed to the public, and settlements between governments and investors are not disclosed. While this is standard practice in many domestic legal battles, it clouds the public's trust in the system. The lack of transparency adds to concerns about an insufficiently democratic approach.

Although the ISDS system bears the brunt of concern and criticism, FDI has its skeptics as well. To attract investment, subnational governments such as provinces, states, and even municipalities often compete in an international marketplace to entice large companies to relocate or build facilities within their jurisdictions. To win this investment, local governments dole out tax breaks and other incentives such as workforce training grants and changes to local regulations. Critics of these policies claim this has developed into an arms race, or a globalized "race to the bottom," where companies seek out the cheapest, most unregulated options available to the detriment of workers and consumers.

Given the tight linkage between investment and trade in modern international commerce, it is inevitable that trade participants will push to include investment rules in trade agreements. The difficulty is striking a balance between the need to attract and facilitate investment without providing it too much regulatory leeway and advantages that are not afforded to domestic companies. The next chapter in the monograph will consider some possibilities for addressing the controversies over ISDS.

Technical barriers to trade

Independent states strive to develop laws and standards to protect their citizens. Yet standards and regulations that are considered appropriate vary from one country to the next. For companies that export to a host of countries, variability in standards creates inefficiencies and hinders growth. If standards are set arbitrarily or are not followed appropriately, they become obstacles to trade and susceptible to abuse by governments hoping to protect domestic industries from competition. But regulations and standards can also be warranted such as guarding consumer health and, increasingly, consumer data. Determining what qualifies as appropriate regulation as opposed to veiled protectionism is more difficult than it may appear.

This problem is at the heart of debates about nontariff measures known as "technical barriers to trade." The term applies to regulations that can deter international commerce, though they may appear "behind the border"—that is, within a country's domestic legal framework, rather than explicitly targeted at imports. These barriers represent a key component in the future development of global trade liberalization.

Technical barriers to trade can take many forms. They can be mundane, such as requiring additional custom checks or queues at the border. This is particularly true for time-sensitive products such as produce, which spoils if not quickly brought to market. These tactics may be conducted under the auspices of protecting consumers from diseased or rotting produce even when clear political considerations are in play, such as when China banned imported fruit from the Philippines as bilateral ties worsened over disputes in the South China Sea.[152]

More commonly, however, the discrepancy between unwarranted barriers to trade and appropriate regulation is less obvious. The case of automobile headlamp regulation in South Korea is a prime example. During the latter half of the 20th century, Korean law prohibited autos that did not meet Korean headlamp safety standards, which included those manufactured in the United States or the European Union.[153] North American and European headlamp safety regulations were deemed too lenient for South Korean standards, which require headlights to automatically adjust based on road conditions.[154] According to the US Department of Commerce, the regulations were only part of an insulated domestic car bias in South Korea—often pursued and supported by the government—which included anti-import sentiments.[155] With pressure from the United States, South Korea began to align its regulations more with European Union and North American standards.[156] Yet these barriers continue to persist. To receive exemption from the Trump administration's steel and aluminum tariffs, South Korea increased the quota of total imported cars that pass North American but not Korean road safety standards.

---

152. This monograph uses the term "technical barriers to trade" expansively. In trade negotiations, some of these barriers could fall under more specific categories such as customs procedures or sanitary and phytosanitary regulation. Yawen Chen and Karl Plume, "China Customs Expands Checks on U.S. Fruit Imports: Sources," Reuters, May 3, 2018, https://www.reuters.com /article/us-usa-trade-china-fruits/chinese-customs-expands-checks-on-u-s -fruit-imports-sources-idUSKBN1I428K.

153. Steven Popper et al., *Measuring Economic Effects of Technical Barriers to Trade on U.S. Exporters* (Arlington, VA: RAND Science and Technology, 2004), 106, https://www.nist.gov/sites/default/files/documents/director /planning/report04-3.pdf.

154. Moon Hee-Chul and Choi Hyung-Jo, "FTA Revisions Lets U.S. Bypass Korean Regulations," *Korean Joongang Daily*, April 11, 2018, http:// koreajoongangdaily.joins.com/news/article/article.aspx?aid=3046761.

155. United States Department of Commerce, *The Compilation of World Motor Import Requirements* (Washington, DC: United States Department of Commerce, Office of Transportation and Machinery, 2011), 46, https://www.trade.gov/td/otm/assets/auto/autos_tradebarriers2011.pdf.

156. United States Trade Representative, *Korea Memorandum of Understanding Regarding Foreign Motor Vehicles* (Washington, DC: United States Trade Representative, Office of Trade Agreements Negotiation and Compliance, October 20, 1998), https://tcc.export.gov /Trade_Agreements/All_Trade_Agreements/exp_005688.asp.

Regulatory frameworks can go beyond specifications for the product and into how the item is manufactured or produced. The ongoing debate between the United States and European Union concerning the cleaning and dressing of poultry products is a clear example. While cleaning poultry with chlorine dioxide and other antimicrobial rinses has been illegal in the European Union since 1997—based on concerns that such pathogen reduction techniques mask a lack of hygiene in poultry processing—the process is allowed under US law.[157] Because of this difference in standards, the European Union imports almost no poultry from the United States even though US-produced poultry has a significant price advantage.[158] The disagreement has led to two WTO cases, and the debate has entered the dialogue around safety standards in TTIP negotiations.[159] Although scientific evidence demonstrates the safety of the US regulations, the European Union has remained staunch in support of its rules, claiming it will not engage in a "race to the bottom" on food standards by overlooking unsanitary production techniques. From the US perspective, this intransigence toward adopting US food standards masks the European Union's protectionist tendencies toward its food sector.

To reduce the number of such disputes and discordant regulations, several WTO agreements attempt to parse differences in standards. Established during the Uruguay Round of negotiations, the Agreement

---

157. Daniel Boffey and Jessica Elgot, "Brussels Attacks Liam Fox's 'Ignorant' Remarks on Chlorinated Chicken," *The Guardian*, July 25, 2017, https://www.theguardian.com/politics/2017/jul/25/brussels-attacks-liam -foxs-ignorant-remarks-chlorinated-chicken-eu-trade-deal-us; George Monbiot, "Chlorinated Chicken? Yes, We Really Can Have Too Much Trade," *The Guardian*, July 25, 2017, https://www.theguardian.com /commentisfree/2017/jul/25/chlorinated-chicken-trade-britain-us-food -standards-globalisation; Tim Josling and Stefan Tangermann, "TTIP and Agriculture: Another Transatlantic Chicken War?" *Choices* 31, no. 2 (2016): 1–7.

158. Renée Johnson, *U.S.-EU Poultry Dispute on the Use of Pathogen Reduction Treatments (PRTs)* (Washington, DC: Congressional Research Service, 2014), http://nationalaglawcenter.org/wp-content/uploads/assets /crs/R40199.pdf.

159. "United States – Measures Affecting Imports of Poultry Products," World Trade Organization, https://www.wto.org/english/tratop_e/dispu_e /cases_e/ds100_e.htm; "European Communities – Certain Measures Affecting Poultry Meat and Poultry Meat Products from the United States," World Trade Organization, https://www.wto.org/english/tratop_e/dispu_e /cases_e/ds389_e.htm.

on Technical Barriers to Trade (TBT) included provisions ensuring that nontariff barriers to trade are removed and that testing and certification procedures for consumer safety would not create unnecessary obstacles.[160] According to the TBT Agreement, WTO members are allowed to adopt standards they consider appropriate so long as they apply the same regulations unilaterally. The agreement also lays out a code of standards of good practice for governments to adopt, which encourages members to adhere to generally recognized international standards and requires them to make transparent regulatory changes.

Developed in conjunction with the TBT Agreement was the Agreement on the Application of Sanitary and Phytosanitary Measures (SPS).[161] Like the TBT Agreement, the SPS Agreement is meant to protect legitimate consumer safety standards for food production while also ensuring that such standards would not be used as a cloak for protectionism.

In subsequent years, trade pacts have built on the foundation of WTO regulation. Most recently, in TPP negotiations, a chapter on technical barriers to trade expanded on the provisions of the TBT Agreement. A regulatory coherence chapter was added that would require TPP members to ensure similarity with US assessment processes to streamline testing and minimize costs.[162] Moreover, a compliance period of six months would allow exporters to adjust to any new regulations in member countries. Most of these provisions have been adopted by TPP-11 in the absence of US involvement.

The emergence of technical barriers to trade means that seemingly obscure discussions about regulatory practice can have important implications for whether US goods are able to enter foreign markets. It also means that simple commitments to lower tariff barriers may be insufficient to guarantee market access.

---

160. "Standards and Safety," World Trade Organization, https://www.wto.org/english/thewto_e/whatis_e/tif_e/agrm4_e.htm.

161. "The WTO Agreement on the Application of Sanitary and Phytosanitary Measures (SPS Agreement)," World Trade Organization, https://www.wto.org/english/tratop_e/sps_e/spsagr_e.htm.

162. "Report of the Industry Trade Advisory Committee on Standards and Technical Barriers to Trade (ITAC 16)" (Advisory Committee Report to the president, Congress and the United States Trade Representative on the Trans-Pacific Partnership Trade Agreement, December 2, 2015), https://ustr.gov/sites/default/files/ITAC-16-Standards-and-Technical-Barriers-to-Trade.pdf.

Intellectual property

Protecting intellectual property (IP) is fundamental to successful free enterprise. A lack of protection disincentivizes companies and individuals from innovation and stalls further technological development, as large-scale investments are vulnerable to theft from competitors.

Likewise, IP protections, much like investor protections, are vital for FDI and international trade. But just as levels of development vary between trading countries, so too do the protections provided for IP and the recourse for those whose property has been stolen.

While trade agreements have incorporated IP chapters for decades, the creation of the WTO in 1994 went beyond the requirements of the GATT and into arenas that had not previously been part of trade-related discussions.

An example of this growing reach of trade came with the establishment of the Agreement on Trade-Related Aspects of Intellectual Property Rights (TRIPS), a pact that requires all WTO countries to uphold minimum standards of IP protection.[163] This provision has become one of the more controversial aspects of the WTO's purview. It not only links a hitherto nontrade issue to the WTO's framework, but it can be seen as favoring multinational corporations over the needs of less-developed countries.

One prominent example of the battleground concerns drug prices. Tight IP protection allows pharmaceutical companies to charge higher prices. That provides an incentive for the companies to undertake costly drug research. The successful drugs cover both their own development cost and the cost of the experiments that failed. Yet costly drugs can have a direct, negative effect on sick patients. It is particularly galling when drug purchasers pay hefty amounts for pills that are cheap to produce (once development costs are ignored). Unlike with tariffs, economic reasoning does not offer clear guidance about optimal policy—how to balance the incentive to innovate against the potential cost to consumers of high prices.

When the WTO's Doha Round kicked off in 2001, a major goal of the agreement was to expand and improve upon the TRIPS Agreement. After numerous unsuccessful negotiating rounds, the talks were sus-

---

163. "Trade-Related Aspects of Intellectual Property Rights," World Trade Organization, https://www.wto.org/english/tratop_e/trips_e/trips_e.htm.

pended. Further implementation and modification of IP considerations have now moved into bilateral and plurilateral trade negotiations.

Questions of IP protection have become particularly intense in US dealings with China. The Trump administration has argued that China's requirement that US companies share proprietary technologies has cost the United States billions of dollars.[164] China's stance has often been that, while it supports the protection of IP rights, existing WTO rules do not require it to spend an inordinate amount on enforcement.

While dealings with China have been particularly heated, IP protection was also prominent in TPP talks and in the renegotiation of NAFTA, where there was a push in the United States to enhance protection of biologics, or new methods of treating disease that go beyond chemicals to include proteins, nucleic acids, or living tissues.[165] The United States has generally pushed for more extensive protection of IP than its developed trading partners prefer.

Advocates argue for the inclusion of IP issues in trade agreements for two reasons. The first is that weak IP protection can preclude trade flows. If a country can import a single movie on a Blu-ray disc and then make as many copies as it likes, millions of dollars of video exports can be lost.

The second is that trade agreements are one of the few enforcement mechanisms with real teeth. Countries can agree on IP practices through separate bodies such as the World Intellectual Property Organization (WIPO), but it is difficult to see how transgressions can be held to account without the ability to punish through trade actions.[166]

National security

The moment it became clear that President Trump intended to take a different and more aggressive approach to trade policy—as opposed

164. United States Trade Representative, *Findings of the Investigation into China's Acts, Policies, and Practices Related to Technology Transfer, Intellectual Property, and Innovation Under Section 301 of the Trade Act of 1974* (Washington, DC: Office of the United States Trade Representative, March 22, 2018), https://ustr.gov/sites/default/files/Section%20301%20FINAL.PDF.
165. "What Are 'Biologics' Questions and Answers," United States Food and Drug Administration, https://www.fda.gov/aboutfda/centersoffices/officeofmedicalproductsandtobacco/cber/ucm133077.htm.
166. See the World Intellectual Property Organization, https://www.wipo.int/portal/en/index.html.

to just rhetoric—was when he proclaimed 25 percent tariffs on imports of steel and 10 percent tariffs on imports of aluminum.[167] Normally, there are two key obstacles to a US president slapping tariffs on imports: WTO constraints on tariff levels and the US Constitution, which grants authority over tariffs to the US Congress.

Trump overcame those obstacles by claiming that the tariffs were necessary for national security. In so doing, he made use of authority that Congress had delegated to the president under Section 232 of the Trade Expansion Act of 1962 during the Cold War.[168] The authority had not been used since 1986 when President Ronald Reagan cited the authority to push for relief for the machine tool industry. In that instance, however, the Reagan administration eschewed tariffs and negotiated "voluntary" quota restrictions on foreign exports—a practice that was subsequently prohibited under global trade rules.[169] Including Reagan's action, there had been 49 petitions for this sort of relief since the Dwight D. Eisenhower administration, but only six positive responses prior to Trump's presidency.[170]

One legal analysis of the legislation gave an example of the sort of national security concern that might arise and justify the use of such tariffs: "Where defense needs are dependent upon the importation of goods by sea, and the sea-lanes are likely to be interdicted by hostile naval forces, it may be impractical to airlift supplies from overseas."[171]

167.   David Lynch and Damian Paletta, "Trump Announces Steel and Aluminum Tariffs Thursday Over Objections from Advisers and Republicans," *The Washington Post*, March 1, 2018, https://www.washingtonpost.com /news/business/wp/2018/03/01/white-house-planning-major-announcement-thursday-on-steel-and-aluminum-imports/?noredirect=on &utm_term=.6ba72cc30b3e.

168.   For a history and analysis, see David D. Knoll, "Section 232 of the Trade Expansion Act of 1962: Industrial Fasteners, Machine Tools and Beyond," *Maryland Journal of International Law* 10, no. 1 (1986), http://digitalcommons.law.umaryland.edu/mjil/vol10/iss1/4. See also "Section 323 Investigations: The Effects of Imports on the National Security," Bureau of Industry and Security, United States Department of Commerce, https://www.bis.doc.gov/232.

169.   Clyde Farnsworth, "Reagan Acts to Restrict Machine Tool Imports," *The New York Times*, May 21, 1986, https://www.nytimes.com/1986/05/21 /business/reagan-acts-to-restrict-machine-tool-imports.html.

170.   Todd Tucker, "Are National Security Tariffs Legal?" *Medium*, February 16, 2018, https://medium.com/@toddntucker/are-national-security-tariffs -legal-2e8b0188a170.

171.   Knoll, "Section 232 of the Trade Expansion Act of 1962," 57.

Another potentially concerning scenario occurred when China became the dominant source of "rare earth material" extraction, processing, and manufacture.[172] What would happen if the United States were cut off from these critical minerals?

Even in such circumstances, it is certainly not clear that trade restrictions are the least painful means of achieving a goal, or if they even help at all. If the concern is having access to a certain quantity of a material in case of an interruption, a stockpile may address the need. If the concern is maintaining domestic production, then a domestic subsidy may be less damaging than protection, particularly because it would not damage industries that use the product by inflicting higher prices.

The national security issue was also considered under the GATT with Article XXI, "Security Exceptions."[173] The article concisely lays out three scenarios under which WTO members might take action to protect essential security interests:

- ▶ Trade in fissionable materials

- ▶ Trade in arms, ammunition, and implements of war

- ▶ Trade in time of war or emergency

In the case of Trump's steel and aluminum tariffs, none of these exceptions applied. Nor did the Department of Commerce report develop a serious argument along the lines of military need.[174] In fact, the Department of Defense sent a memorandum noting that "US military requirements for steel and aluminum each only represent about 3 percent

---

172. See a detailed study by David An, "Critical Rare Earths, National Security, and U.S.-China Interactions" (PhD diss., Pardee RAND Graduate School, 2014), https://www.rand.org/pubs/rgs_dissertations/RGSD337.html.

173. World Trade Organization, "Article XXI: Security Exceptions," in *General Agreement on Tariffs and Trade (GATT)* (Geneva: World Trade Organization), https://www.wto.org/english/res_e/booksp_e/gatt_ai_e /art21_e.pdf.

174. Phil Levy, "The Commerce Department Makes a Feeble National Security Plea for Steel Protection," *Forbes*, February 16, 2018, https://www.forbes .com/sites/phillevy/2018/02/16/the-commerce-departments-feeble- national-security-plea-for-steel-protection/#4abe5bad42dc.

of US production." It saw no problem acquiring the steel or aluminum necessary to meet national defense requirements.[175]

The defense memo instead highlighted a potentially serious national security cost of the tariff actions: "DoD continues to be concerned about the negative impact on our key allies." As it played out, the imposition of the tariffs caused at least two serious problems with allies. First, modern production is often integrated across national borders. The US aluminum industry, for example, is highly integrated with the Canadian aluminum industry, with parts being shipped across the border for finishing and modification.

Second, the steel action predominantly hit US allies, particularly once the Trump administration removed the exclusions it had initially offered countries such as Canada, Mexico, and the European Union. The Department of State maintains a list of the countries with which the United States has collective defense arrangements.[176] Using that list, six of the top eight steel suppliers to the United States in 2017 were defense allies. (The exceptions were #4 Mexico and #5 Russia. Canada was #1.) While the Trump administration tried to portray China as the true target of the action, China was the #11 supplier, providing just under 2.2 percent of reported imports. This was because more than 90 percent of US steel imports from China were already subject to special protection (generally AD/CVD).[177] Thus, just as the Department of Defense feared, the action strained important security alliances.

The rationale used by the Trump administration was to equate "economic security" with "national security." This implied that what was good for the steel industry would also be good for economic security and therefore national security. But the Trump administration did not grapple with the trade-off between steel-producing and steel-using

---

175. "Response to Steel and Aluminum Policy Recommendations" (memorandum from the United States Department of Defense to the United States Department of Commerce), https://www.commerce.gov/sites/default/files/department_of_defense_memo_response_to_steel_and_aluminum_policy_recommendations.pdf.

176. "U.S. Collective Defense Arrangements," United States Department of State, last modified 2004, https://www.state.gov/s/l/treaty/collectivedefense.

177. Chad Bown, "Trump's Steel and Aluminum Tariffs Are Counterproductive. Here Are 5 More Things You Need to Know," *Trade & Investment Policy Watch* (blog), Washington, DC: Peterson Institute for International Economics, March 7, 2018, https://piie.com/blogs/trade-investment-policy-watch/trumps-steel-and-aluminum-tariffs-are-counterproductive-here-are.

industries. Raw steel and aluminum are generally not used in defense. They become useful for weapons or transport when transformed through manufacturing. In the United States, the steel production industry employs 140,000 workers. There are roughly 2 million employed in industries that heavily use steel.[178] Those industries processing steel and aluminum have been hurt, presumably damaging the country's economic security. Additionally, other industries were hurt through the inevitable retaliation by aggrieved trading partners. This is one illustration of the more complicated effects of protection in an era of supply chains.

In fact, the Trump administration launched a follow-on Section 232 investigation of autos, a sector that is wholly constructed around integrated supply chains.[179] In response to the investigation, an alliance of top auto manufacturers wrote: "We believe the resulting impact of tariffs on imported vehicles and vehicle components will ultimately harm US economic security and weaken our national security. The potential negative ramifications of such tariffs to the nation's auto industry, consumers, and overall US economy are real."[180]

An additional difficulty with the rationale that does not link the trade action to a well-specified military need is that it becomes flexible enough to serve as an excuse for virtually any protection.

The potential damage from a loose rationale extends to other countries and the WTO. Multiple countries filed disputes against the United States in the wake of the steel and aluminum tariffs under Section 232. Given the limited nature of the exception described in Article XXI, they would seem to have a legitimate complaint, as none of the specifics apply. Yet the United States has argued that Article XXI should be

---

178. Lydia Cox and Kadee Russ, "Will Steel Tariffs Put U.S. Jobs at Risk?" *Econofact*, February 26, 2018, https://econofact.org/will-steel-tariffs-put-u-s-jobs-at-risk.

179. Phil Levy, "Et Tu, Autos? The Case for National Security Tariffs Is Weak," *Forbes*, May 24, 2018, https://www.forbes.com/sites/phillevy/2018/05/24/et-tu-autos-more-national-security-tariffs/#167ebb1b59b4.

180. "AutoAlliance232Comments_FINAL" (Auto Alliance letter to Secretary Wilbur Ross, United States Department of Commerce, June 27, 2018), 3, https://www.regulations.gov/document?D=DOC-2018-0002-1834.

"self-judging"—the country adopting the exception should get to judge whether it is legitimate.[181]

This leaves the WTO in a very dangerous situation as the disputes proceed. If it finds that the United States was justified in imposing steel and aluminum protection, the implication will be that any country can break any WTO promise it pleases so long as it is willing to cry "national security." Alternatively, if the panel rules against the United States, there will be a political firestorm over an international institution sitting in judgment of US national security needs. This conundrum was a major reason why invoking the national security exception at the WTO had previously been seen as taboo.

Labor and environmental issues

As noted earlier in the history of trade, labor and environmental issues claimed a prominent spot in US trade policy debates in the early 1990s around the time the original NAFTA was signed. The theories behind the inclusion of the two topics were fairly similar. In each case, groups concerned about the removal of trade barriers worried that they would spur a global "race to the bottom" in both environmental and labor standards.

In the case of labor, the fear was that if manufacturing could take place in a country that paid workers $4 per hour (or less), then factories would all shut down and relocate to the sites with the lowest wages.

This fear is heavily based on the misconception that labor productivity is identical the world over. Suppose, instead, that a US worker turns out six times as many units in an hour as a Mexican worker. In that case, a manufacturer should be willing to pay the US worker up to six times as much as the Mexican worker. That ratio, in fact, was roughly the estimate of productivity and wage differences between the United States and Mexico at the time of NAFTA's initial adoption.

As with IP, there were both direct concerns about how trade might affect wages as well as the possibility of using the signing of a trade agreement as an occasion to pressure the trading partner to adopt standards on wages, union organization, or worker safety organization

---

181. Krysztof Pelc, "The U.S. Broke a Huge Global Trade Taboo. Here's Why Trump's Move Might Be Legal," *The Washington Post*, June 7, 2018, https://www.washingtonpost.com/news/monkey-cage/wp/2018/06/07/the -u-s-broke-a-huge-global-trade-taboo-heres-why-trumps-move-might-be -legal/?utm_term=.22472b8c4d33.

that US groups preferred. Whether or not this push for higher standards is meant altruistically, it is often perceived as an attack by developing countries. Higher standards tend to be costly. The United States raised its labor standards only as it developed, with notorious stories about the mistreatment of labor abundant at the beginning of the 20th century.

Developing countries with low average wages and productivity are often acutely aware of the difficulties of producing there (e.g., poor infrastructure, difficult transportation, problematic politics). They see the move to raise wages or standards by fiat as an attempt to kill their industry and eliminate the one advantage that might allow them to be competitive.

The concerns about the environment are similar. The theory is that lax environmental regulation will reduce business costs and attract investment. This will mean either manufacturing relocation to places with weak regulation or an incentive to weaken existing regulation in the United States. The evidence of trade's effect is mixed. People tend to demand higher environmental quality as they grow wealthier.[182] Further, trade can result in a propagation of high environmental standards—a "race to the top."[183]

One difficulty with including environmental standards in trade agreements is that no universal agreement exists on which levels of environmental protection are appropriate. There are certainly sharp differences between developed and developing countries, but there are also notable contrasts between countries at comparable levels of development such as the United States and the European Union.

In the wake of the original environmental and labor side letters to NAFTA, the enforceability of labor and environmental provisions became a highly divisive issue in the United States. Democrats insisted on strong provisions as an important prerequisite to backing a deal.

---

182. This is sometimes described as an "environmental Kuznets curve." The idea is that initially development and manufacturing degrade the environment, but eventually as income grows, the desire for environmental quality prompts stronger regulation. For more on the environmental Kuznets curve, see Dimitra Kaika and Efthimios Zervas, "The Environmental Kuznets Curve (EKC) Theory—Part A: Concept, Causes and the CO2 Emissions Case," *ScienceDirect* 62 (November 2013): 1392–402, https://doi.org/10.1016/j.enpol.2013.07.131.

183. Eri Saikawa, "Policy Diffusion of Emission Standards Is There a Race to the Top?" *World Politics* 65, no. 1 (2013): 1–33. http://doi.org/10.1017/S0043887112000238.

Republicans worried that trade agreements might serve as a backdoor means of imposing regulatory restrictions that would otherwise not gain support in Congress.

Labor and environmental issues came to the policy forefront in 2007 after Democrats took control of the House of Representatives in the 2006 midterm elections. President Bush had four trade agreements pending that he hoped to pass with Colombia, Panama, Peru, and South Korea. To pass, they needed to move first through the House.

The Bush administration negotiated with the new Democratic House leadership, announcing a deal on May 10, 2007, that was intended to deliver bipartisan support for FTAs.[184] Designed to act as a template for the four FTAs under consideration or in negotiation at the time, the May 10th Agreement focused mainly on labor and environmental protections that had been long-standing Democratic issues.[185]

The May 10th Agreement required countries participating in FTAs with the United States to comply with the International Labour Organization (ILO) standards, much like previous arrangements that demanded adherence to the Generalized System of Preferences.[186] But there were still limitations: any violation would be subject to litigation only if it occurred in a manner affecting trade or investment, ruling out labor concerns arising from firms that did not export or import.[187] Moreover, the labor disputes would be subject to the same dispute settlement procedures as commercial trade disputes.

On environmental matters, the deal required compliance with several multilateral environmental agreements (MEAs), each containing specific environmental guidelines.[188] The agreement also specified that MEA environmental standards were to be incorporated into the text

---

184. Sungjoon Cho, "The Bush Administration and Democrats Reach a Bipartisan Deal on Trade Policy," *American Society of International Law* 11, no. 15 (May 31, 2007), https://www.asil.org/insights/volume/11/issue/15/bush-administration-and-democrats-reach-bipartisan-deal-trade-policy.

185. Steven Weisman, "Bush and Democrats in Accord on Trade Deals," *The New York Times*, May 11, 2007, https://www.nytimes.com/2007/05/11/business/11trade.html.

186. For more information on the International Labour Organization, visit http://www.ilo.org/global/about-the-ilo/lang--en/index.htm.

187. "Bipartisan Trade Deal," Office of the United States Trade Representative.

188. "Bipartisan Trade Deal," Office of the United States Trade Representative. The list includes agreements such as the Convention of International Trade in Endangered Species and the Montreal Protocol on Ozone Depleting Substances.

of trade agreements, subjecting any violation—just as with labor pro-visions—to the same dispute settlement procedure as a commercial trade dispute.[189]

As a means to ensure bipartisan support for trade deals, the May 10th Agreement failed. Only the Peru FTA came to a vote, and it had appeared likely to pass in any case.[190]

Years later, the negotiated TPP included a labor chapter that called for all participating countries to adopt labor rights outlined in the ILO standards and stipulated the development of safety and health stan-dards.[191] That proved insufficient to win bipartisan support.

The Trump administration claimed to strengthen labor and environ-mental provisions even further in its renegotiated NAFTA. Whether this is sufficient to win Democratic support remains to be seen. Early indica-tions are that Democratic leaders have found enforcement provisions to be insufficient.[192]

Sovereignty, dispute settlement, and overreach

One reason that issues such as IP, labor, and environmental regula-tion have ended up on the agenda of global trade negotiations is the perceived success of the WTO at enforcing its rules. In contrast, what power do international organizations such as the WIPO or the ILO have if members misbehave?

The perception is that trade agreements are enforced by the threat of sanctions. This provides a more persuasive incentive against mis-behavior. Yet it also raises questions about whether such actions are infringements on national sovereignty.[193]

---

189. "Bipartisan Trade Deal," Office of the United States Trade Representative.
190. It was supported by Charlie Rangel (D-NY), who was then Chairman of the Ways & Means Committee.
191. "Consolidated TPP Text – Chapter 19 – Labour," Government of Canada, updated December 6, 2016, https://international.gc.ca/trade-commerce /trade-agreements-accords-commerciaux/agr-acc/tpp-ptp/text-texte/19 .aspx?lang=eng.
192. Sabrina Rodriguez, "Pelosi Casts Doubt on Passage of Trump's New NAFTA Without Changes," *Politico*, December 6, 2018, https://www.politico .com/story/2018/12/06/pelosi-casts-doubt-on-trumps-usmca-passage -without-changes-1014361.
193. Greg Rushford, "Trump's War on the WTO," *The Wall Street Journal*, July 4, 2018, https://www.wsj.com/articles/trumps-war-on-the-wto-1530723098.

To delve into these questions, we begin with the legal status of trade agreements in the United States and proceed to the functioning of dispute settlement mechanisms.

In the United States, trade agreements are not treaties. They are domestic laws. Once a president's administration strikes a trade deal with negotiating partners, it needs to provide Congress with a bill known as "implementing legislation." As described earlier, such bills can move through the House and Senate in a privileged fashion, immune from tabling, amendment, or filibuster. But, ultimately, they require majority votes in the House and Senate and the president's signature, just like any other law. Thus, the legal force of these agreements is entirely domestic and derives from the unassailability of US national sovereignty.

While an agreement such as NAFTA obviously emanated from a three-way negotiation, it was the choice of the US Congress whether to adopt it. This is not an empty choice. In the case of TPP, the US Trade Representative signed the deal in February 2016, but it was never submitted to Congress as implementing legislation. That meant that it had no force whatsoever in the United States and did not change US policy.

That sovereignty is undimmed in the case of a dispute. Although trade agreements such as NAFTA have their own dispute settlement mechanisms, in the interests of being precise, we will focus on the most prominent dispute settlement mechanism—that of the WTO.[194] Further, we can consider an active case: the complaints filed against the United States for its Section 232 national security tariffs on steel and aluminum.

The issue is not whether such action violated an abstract conception of free trade. No WTO prosecutor presses such cases. Instead, the question is whether the United States broke its side of a bargain. In previous negotiating rounds, the United States committed to not raise its tariffs on steel, for example, above zero.[195] The presumption is that this promise was valuable to US trading partners and that they had reciprocally offered lowered tariffs or other concessions in return.

---

194. For abundant information, including links to cases, see "Dispute Settlement," World Trade Organization, https://www.wto.org/english/tratop_e/dispu_e/dispu_e.htm.

195. One bound rate in the broad steel category is as high as 5.8 percent (spiegeleisen containing by weight more than 90 percent of silicon), but most tariff lines are bound at zero. The question, in any case, would be whether the United States had exceeded its bound tariff levels.

A case starts when a country files a complaint at the WTO, as Canada did against the United States for steel on June 6, 2018.[196] The complaint begins as a request for consultations. If the dispute is not resolved through consultations after a specified period, a dispute settlement panel is appointed, consisting of impartial trade experts. This panel hears arguments from the involved countries and ultimately issues a report detailing its findings. The panel in the Canadian/US steel case is primarily concerned with whether the United States broke its promise, which will hinge on whether the imposition of tariffs was justified under GATT Article XXI (described above).

Under the WTO, a panel finding is adopted unless there is a unanimous agreement to reject it (the weaker system under the GATT had the reverse, requiring unanimous support to adopt). The WTO also has an appellate body to which a losing party can appeal.

For the sake of argument, let's assume the panel and appellate body both find that the United States was not justified in imposing the steel tariffs. There are then three possible outcomes:

1. The United States could remove the steel tariffs. This is what the Bush administration did when it received such a finding on its steel safeguard action in 2003.

2. The United States could offer compensation to Canada. This could be financial or some equally valuable concession in exchange. This is relatively rare.

3. Canada could authorize withdrawing a concession of equivalent value. This would be depicted as retaliation, but the idea is to unwind the original deal.

The essential role of the WTO dispute settlement mechanism is to be an independent arbiter of whether rules were broken and, if so, how bad the damage was. The idea is not to force nations to comply—a power it does not possess—but rather to prevent escalating retaliation in which countries disagree over the extent of damage and start retaliating against retaliation.

---

196. World Trade Organization, *United States – Certain Measures on Steel and Aluminum Products – Request for Consultations by Canada* (Geneva: World Trade Organization, June 6, 2018), https://docs.wto.org/dol2fe /Pages/FE_Search/FE_S_S006.aspx?Query=(%20@Symbol=%20(wt /ds550/1%20))&Language=ENGLISH&Context=FormerScriptedSearch &languageUIChanged=true.

On the question of sovereignty, the key point is that the United States retains full sovereignty throughout the process. In no way can the WTO compel the United States to act. True, if the United States chooses not to act, other countries can choose to raise tariffs of their own, but that is their sovereign right.[197]

Nevertheless, the WTO dispute settlement mechanism is under threat, in part because the United States has been blocking new appointments to the Appellate Body and the number of judges is quickly dwindling to an unsustainable number.[198]

A key objection to the dispute settlement mechanism, voiced by US Trade Representative Robert Lighthizer, is that dispute settlement panels have been guilty of overreach, finding violations that were not really in the initial agreements.

There may be some merit to such accusations. The difficulty facing the WTO is that its legislative side has not kept up with its judicial side. The agreements on which panels and appellate bodies are drawing were set in the 1990s. Decades on, obvious gaps exist in the coverage of international commercial agreements, such as recent trade agreements' attempts to regulate e-commerce. Any judicial system plays the role of applying abstract rules to particular cases. Ideally, the rules are refreshed over time, so they remain readily applicable and relevant.

The solution to potential judicial overreach at the WTO is not to dismantle the dispute settlement system, as the Trump administration has been attempting. It is to reach new political agreements (trade deals) between the sovereign trading nations.

---

197. In the case of the Section 232 tariffs, the retaliation question was murkier since many countries chose to treat the US protection as a safeguard action and not wait for the WTO dispute settlement process to apply their own retaliation. The United States has argued such retaliation is itself a violation of WTO rules. See United States Trade Representative, "Statement by Ambassador Robert E. Lighthizer on Retaliatory Duties" (press release, Washington, DC: Office of the United States Trade Representative, June 2018), https://ustr.gov/about-us/policy-offices/press -office/press-releases/2018/june/statement-ambassador-robert-e.
198. Josh Wingrove and Yako Takeo, "Gears of WTO Could Soon Halt Amid U.S. Concerns, Canada Warns," *Bloomberg*, January 20, 2019, https://www.bloomberg.com/news/articles/2019-01-20/gears-of-wto-could -soon-halt-amid-u-s-concerns-canada-warns.

Chapter IV: A way forward on trade policy

President Trump took office with the promise that striking new trade deals would be easy. That has not proven to be the case. Near the midway point of his first term, his administration had reached tentative understandings with South Korea and Mexico but not new trade agreements. And those tentative deals were relatively minor revisions of trade agreements struck by his predecessors.[199]

To be fair, President Obama had made similar calls for radical change in 2008, only to pass the Colombia, Korea, and Panama FTAs that had been negotiated by his predecessor with minimal changes. While TPP certainly covered new territory, as in its treatment of SOEs, its negotiation looked more like a continuation of pre-existing trends than a radical departure. It also drew fire from many of the same opponents who had criticized earlier deals.[200]

This raises a fundamental question: do trade deals evolve gradually because successive denizens of the White House all share the same philosophical bent, or do the deals look similar because they are shaped by the same forces? The public presumption has been the former, which has led to ever more strident critiques of trade deals on the presidential campaign trail, as candidates try to prove that only *they* are sufficiently critical of existing trade policy to be credible in their promises to effect change. The clear differences in political philosophies between Clinton, Bush, Obama, and Trump that have coexisted with reasonable continuity in the shape of concluded trade agreements suggest the importance of the shaping forces.

---

199. Jeffrey Schott and Euijin Jung, "KORUS Amendments: Minor Adjustments Fixed What Trump Called 'Horrible Trade Deal" (policy brief, Washington, DC: Peterson Institute for International Economics, November 2018), https://piie.com/system/files/documents/pb18-22.pdf.

200. Catherine Ho, "Industry, Labor and Environmental Groups Gear Up to Oppose TPP Trade Deal," *The Washington Post*, October 6, 2015, https://www.washingtonpost.com/news/powerpost/wp/2015/10/06/industry-labor-and-environmental-groups-gear-up-to-oppose-tpp-trade-deal/?utm_term=.04f728ac582a.

The first section of this chapter considers some of those forces, which have effectively constrained the approach to US trade agreements. The next section moves on to consider some of the options in terms of the negotiating forum—whether trade deals can best be struck issue by issue or in broad deals, bilaterally or in global rounds. The final section looks at some of the most controversial topics in trade agreements and asks which ones are most amenable to a different approach.

Pressures shaping trade agreements

Trading partners

First and foremost among the forces shaping US trade agreements are US trading partners. The internal political divisions in the United States over trade policy have been so sharp in recent decades that it is tempting to conclude that internal agreement is all that matters. Instead, trade negotiations fit the pattern of what Robert Putnam once described as a "two-level game."[201] To pull it off, one needs to succeed at both the domestic level and the international level, and the two are interconnected.

This necessarily constrains the sorts of trade policy stances the United States can take in negotiations. The United States is a formidable economic power with ample leverage, but neither its power nor its leverage is unlimited. To some extent, the US perception that it could demand whatever it liked in international trade deals stems from a succession of deals with smaller countries, such as Oman, Panama, and Peru. In such cases, the United States largely *could* demand what it liked. That was not true with Australia, Canada, Japan, or the European Union.

One thing that all trading partners tend to demand is that policies apply symmetrically. Thus, if there is a ban on all subsidies to a trading partner's domestic industries, the United States has to be willing to

---

201. Robert Putnam, "Diplomacy and Domestic Politics: The Logic of Two-Level Games," *International Organization* 42, no. 3 (1988): 427–60, http://www.jstor.org/stable/2706785.

follow the same rules—which often severely constrains the sorts of proposals the United States is willing to put forth.[202]

International standard

A second set of pressures comes from US companies that do business around the world. The United States accounts for roughly 25 percent of world economic output, but that means there's still a large share of the world's consumers to access beyond US borders.[203] US businesses have been very successful at working in those markets, ranking No. 2 globally in merchandise exports and No. 1 globally in the export of commercial services.[204]

But it is difficult for businesses if they face different sets of rules in each market in which they operate. One could have such a scenario if each successive US president were to completely reinvent the shape of US trade agreements. To avoid this, leading US exporters tend to push for new trade agreements to be broadly similar to old ones.

Members of Congress

There is a similar pressure to minimize changes that comes from the US Congress. As discussed above, Congress ultimately approves or rejects trade agreements. Those agreements, covering the range of topics discussed in the previous section (and more) in great detail, can be exceedingly complex. The continuity means that members and staff can focus on the limited number of changes that US negotiators will highlight for them—effectively a "track changes" approach to trade policy.

In some ways, this approach to honoring traditions in trade policy plays the same role as honoring established traditions in law or other

---

202. In trade parlance, "offensive interests" are what one country asks of another country and "defensive interests" are what the other country asks in return. There was a stark example of the push for symmetry in October 2017 when the Trump administration tried to propose new rules of origin for autos that specifically mandated a level of *US* content. The objectionable proposal seemed to give way to a wage requirement, which at least appears to be uniformly applied across countries even though it will disproportionately affect Mexico.

203. Robbie Gramer, "Infographic: Here's How the Global GDP Is Divvied Up," *Foreign Policy*, February 24, 2017, https://foreignpolicy.com/2017/02/24 /infographic-heres-how-the-global-gdp-is-divvied-up.

204. "United States of America," World Trade Organization, http://stat.wto.org /CountryProfile/WSDBCountryPFView.aspx?Language=E&Country=US.

fields. It saves participants from having to refight old fights every time.
The effect is to push toward trade agreements that closely resemble
each other.

Business, agriculture, labor, consumers

Ultimately, trade agreements pass Congress if they enjoy sufficient
support from the American public. While public opinion is an important
part of that, the practical demands of legislating tend to mean that there
must be groups such as business associations, consumer groups, farmers, or organized labor, who feel *strongly* that they need the trade deal
under discussion. These groups then work to persuade legislators.

This idea of building support for the trial by Congress is usually at
the forefront of US negotiators' thinking. For decades, the US Trade
Representative has maintained a system of outside advisory groups for
exactly this purpose: to tap into the sentiment of key groups during the
negotiating process.

This played a critical role in the inclusion of IP rights in the Uruguay
Round of global trade talks in the mid-1990s. The question of inclusion
was a topic on which economists had decidedly mixed feelings. Not
only was there no clear economic or political answer about the appropriate level of IP protection, but it was a notable move away from border
barriers and into a domain that had traditionally been part of domestic
regulation.

But US trade strategists were aware of how difficult it would be to
pass a trade agreement through Congress with widespread but mild
approval. It would be dramatically easier if certain groups felt they *had*
to have the deal. Some key US industries—pharmaceuticals, motion pic-
tures, the recording industry, software—all rely heavily on IP protection.
The inclusion of the topic in the Uruguay Round helped make these
groups strong advocates.

As to the pressures for continuity in US trade agreements, the key
point is that these interests often do not change dramatically over time.
The pharmaceutical industry is still very much in favor of strong IP protection, just as US businesses that invest overseas are strongly in favor
of ISDS. Most clauses in trade deals have at least one constituent who
favors that clause's inclusion. This means that proposed radical changes
in agreements are likely to incur opposition from those who do not want
to see their favored clauses cut.

What would bring about a shift?

With all these forces pushing new trade agreements to look like older trade agreements, how can trade policy ever change? There are at least three prominent ways.

First, new issues can come onto the trade agenda. In the early years of the GATT, legislated tariffs were the main barriers to market access, so they were the focus of trade deals. As more and more countries turned to AD/CVD measures to restrict trade, those topics worked their way onto the trade agenda (under the "rules" negotiations) in the 1970s. As trade in services became easier to conduct internationally and a more important part of economic activity, it came onto the agenda in the 1990s (the General Agreement on Trade in Services). In a similar vein, electronic commerce was a nonissue at the time of the Uruguay Round negotiations, but it was one of the chapters of TPP.

Second, there can be revised thinking about how trade rules work. Rules that seemed clear when they were written may prove excessively vague in practice. Regulatory approaches may be contradicted by subsequent scientific findings. Or groups that thought they needed a certain provision for their protection later found it was unnecessary. One interesting feature of the push to renegotiate NAFTA was the widespread consensus that it needed updating. This was partly a reflection of new issues that the old agreement had failed to foresee, but also of better understanding gained over a quarter-century of use.

Third, there could be a shift in supporting coalitions. The cumulation of each of the business, agriculture, consumer, or labor groups pushing for an agreement creates a coalition backing any given trade deal. Usually, a similar coalition will oppose an agreement. The goal of a president pushing a trade deal is to garner 218 votes in favor in the House and 51 in the Senate. Those congressional votes are generally swayed by the opinions of their key constituents. It is certainly possible that more than one coalition could deliver majority support. But that is the key question that administration trade policy strategists usually ask: if they change positions on a certain issue, how many votes will they gain and how many will they lose?

The calculus is whether critics of an existing approach to trade agreements will support the broader trade package if the offending approach is changed. If so, the critics have a fighting chance of getting their way. If, instead, the change still leaves them opposed to the broader deal, only less so, then the change will likely appear to be a political loser. The implication for those who object to US trade policies is that it is essential to offer a viable alternative vision.

Negotiating forum

Before turning to particular issues that critics have raised and exploring whether alternative approaches seem viable, there is the additional question of the forum in which trade discussions should take place. This has been a point of sharp disagreement between Trump, who favors bilateral discussions, and many trade economists, who tend to favor multilateral talks. But the issue actually predates the Trump administration by more than a decade.[205] The difficulties of reaching a consensus among the 164 members of the WTO across the ever-expanding universe of trade policy issues led to serious consideration of alternative approaches.[206]

The baseline disposition of economists toward broad, multilateral rules is based both on the arguments for simplicity and uniformity given above as well as the fundamental belief in the efficiency and fairness in global production. The idea is that if the same trade barriers apply to all potential supplying countries, a buyer will purchase from whichever country can make the good at the least expense. Economists usually think such cost advantages come from either a technological edge or the endowment of relevant inputs to the production process.[207] Many trade complaints revolve around the idea of *unfair* cost advantages due to factors such as inadequate regulation or subsidies. Ideally, those standards of fairness would be agreed upon at a multilateral level.

However, impasses arise in multilateral negotiations. They have led key participants, certainly including the United States, to look for alternatives.

---

205. Philip I. Levy, "Do We Need an Undertaker for the Single Undertaking? Considering the Angles of Variable Geometry," in *Economic Development & Multilateral Trade Cooperation*, eds. Simon J. Evenett and Bernard M. Hoekman (Washington, DC: The World Bank; New York: Palgrave MacMillan, 2006), 419–37.

206. "Members and Observers," World Trade Organization.

207. As an example of endowments, it is dramatically easier and cheaper to grow pineapples in Costa Rica than in Canada because of the climate. Canada, because of its natural resources, has an advantage in generating hydropower, which has proven useful for the production of aluminum, among other things.

Issue or broad-based?

One prominent alternative has been to explore the idea of narrower trade negotiations. Whereas the last rounds of GATT talks featured a full panoply of negotiating issues, why not avoid the complexity of such broad rounds and just take on a limited number? This was something the Clinton administration tried in the immediate wake of the Uruguay Round deal with an agreement on information technology.[208] It is also something the Trump administration has discussed in its dealings with Europe.[209]

The principal problem with a single-issue negotiation is that there may be insufficient scope to strike a deal. As an illustration, suppose the European Union is interested in exporting cars into the United States. The United States, in turn, cares more about exporting machine tools into Europe. If talks are limited to the auto sector, Europe will be the demandeur and the United States will be the demandee. It is unlikely they will find a mutually agreeable deal in such narrow talks, whereas broader talks on industrial tariffs (including machine tools) would allow for the requisite trade-offs.

Bilateral, plurilateral, or multilateral?

If limiting issues is one way of simplifying otherwise complex negotiations, another is by limiting the number of countries participating. Trump has been particularly supportive of bilateral negotiations, arguing that a bilateral setting maximizes US leverage in talks.[210]

This is not necessarily true for at least two different reasons. First, while bilateral talks can suffice for tariff setting, a bilateral deal can look much less appealing than a broader deal when it comes to issues such as rules of origin or setting standards. If a country's businesses can run supply chains across multiple countries and still qualify for preferential

---

208. "Information Technology Agreement," World Trade Organization, https://www.wto.org/english/tratop_e/inftec_e/inftec_e.htm.

209. Hans von der Burchard, Megan Cassella, and Ginger Hervey, "A New Approach to EU-US Trade: Less Is More," *Politico*, September 17, 2018, https://www.politico.eu/article/donald-trump-eu-eye-trade-low-hanging -fruit.

210. Geoffrey Gertz, "What Will Trump's Embrace of Bilateralism Mean for America's Trade Partners?" The Brookings Institute, February 8, 2017, https://www.brookings.edu/blog/future-development/2017/02/08/what -will-trumps-embrace-of-bilateralism-mean-for-americas-trade-partners.

tariff treatment, that opens up substantially greater possibilities than a series of bilateral pairings for a number of reasons.[211] The second big advantage of broader deals is they can allow opportunities to balance a deal that would not exist in narrower talks. For example, suppose Canada had requests only of the United States, the United States had requests only of Japan, and Japan had requests only of Canada. Finding a bilateral deal that would satisfy participants might be impossible, but finding a workable package among the three could be more straightforward and workable.

On top of these considerations, bilateral talks pose much greater logistical demands in negotiation. While three countries would have to conclude three bilateral deals in lieu of a single trilateral one, the complications mount rapidly as the number of countries increases. For the 12 countries of the original TPP, for example, there would be 66 bilateral pairings instead of the single set of regional talks.

Such considerations may have contributed to Japan's recent enthusiasm for the broader TPP and its lack of interest in a bilateral FTA with the United States.[212]

While the United States might not worry much about the need for bilateral negotiations between Peru and Brunei, each US trade deal that has to move through Congress incurs a substantial fixed cost. No matter how big or small the deal, it must follow the notification procedures set out by TPA legislation, be analyzed by the USITC, and receive committee and floor consideration in the House and the Senate. Given the rigors of the process, only three such deals have made it through Congress in the last decade.[213] This provides a political efficiency argument to complement the economic rationale for striking broader deals.

Thus, there is a trade-off. Broad negotiations are great for economic and political efficiency, but the downside can be complex, difficult, protracted negotiations and the problem of holdout countries.

---

211.   The ability to count parts from multiple countries in meeting rules of origin in an FTA is known as "cumulation." For more information, see "Cumulations," European Commission, http://trade.ec.europa.eu /tradehelp/cumulation.

212.   "Japan to Resist Bilateral Trade Deal with US and Push for TPP," *The Straits Times*, July 24, 2018, https://www.straitstimes.com/asia/east-asia/japan -to-resist-bilateral-trade-deal-with-us-and-push-for-tpp.

213.   Colombia, Panama, and South Korea were each negotiated under the George W. Bush administration and passed in 2011 under the Obama administration.

Smaller deals can be sought with willing countries to get around the holdouts, but can be time intensive in total and, unless carefully coordinated, can result in a hodgepodge of conflicting rules that could disadvantage US companies trying to trade around the world.

Brexit

Beyond such general considerations of how trade negotiations might be shaped, some particular options deserve brief consideration, as they can highlight pervasive issues. One option that has piqued popular interest in US trade policy circles is the idea of a bilateral trade deal with the United Kingdom. When the United Kingdom voted to pull out of its membership in the European Union (Brexit), one rationale was that it would then be free to seek trade deals around the world. There was some sentiment among Brexit advocates that the United Kingdom had been inhibited by the more protectionist stances of some of its EU partners such as France. The idea of an FTA with the United States seemed natural, given the special relationship between the two countries.

Two major obstacles stand in the way of such a deal. First, there is the question of what relationship the United Kingdom will have with the remainder of the European Union. If UK trade rules differ in any significant way from those of the European Union, it will require new customs border checks to be created where none presently exist. That can be particularly problematic when it comes to Ireland, an island that currently has no hard border between Northern Ireland, a part of the United Kingdom, and the Republic of Ireland, a member of the European Union.[214] While the United Kingdom might try to use broader WTO rules about tariff levels to keep the Irish border relatively open, those do not provide much help when it comes to critical UK sectors such as financial services. These strong pressures include a total of £615 billion of trade between the United Kingdom and the European Union on an annual basis.[215] There are strong economic pressures on the United Kingdom to maintain trade policies in line with the European Union, which could preclude a separate and different deal with the United States.

---

214. Phil Levy, "With Brexit, President Trump Actually Gets It Right on Trade," *Forbes*, July 14, 2018, https://www.forbes.com/sites/phillevy/2018/07/14/brexit-president-trump-gets-it-right-on-trade/#8adf663a9f01.

215. 2017 total. See "Statistics on UK-EU Trade" (briefing paper, number 7851, House of Commons Library, January 11, 2019), https://researchbriefings.files.parliament.uk/documents/CBP-7851/CBP-7851.pdf.

The second big obstacle has to do with the role of precedent in US trade agreements—the "track changes" approach described above. While the United Kingdom might seem to resemble the United States as a developed and relatively open economy, any new trade agreement between the two would still be a battleground for fights over the treatment of labor, environmental, and health regulation. Some of these fights would involve features of the UK economy, while others would be laying down markers for future trade fights. Treatment of ILO labor rights declarations would be an example of the latter. Treatment of genetically modified foods would be an example of the former.

An FTA between the United States and the United Kingdom is possible, but there is no reason to expect it would be easy.

Europe

In the second Obama administration, the United States engaged the European Union in talks to create TTIP. The talks did not conclude by the end of Obama's term, and the Trump administration appears to have set them aside, preferring its own approach. In July 2018 the Trump administration launched a vague initiative to begin talks with the European Union on a trade deal, though it remains to be seen what form it might take.

The idea of a trade agreement between the United States and the European Union raises two interesting challenges to striking modern trade deals. The first plagued TTIP negotiations and can be thought of as the "lack of low-hanging fruit." Frequently, trade negotiations begin with countries working through standard, predictable issues as they build confidence with each other. The problem for the United States and the European Union was that they had already engaged in eight rounds of GATT talks with one another as well as multiple rounds of bilateral dealings where irritants were removed.[216] Thus, the low-hanging fruit had already been picked clean. The remaining issues were all either ones that had defied solution for decades or new issues such as digital privacy, which proved no easier. While both sides very much liked the idea of striking a deal in the abstract, the specifics proved dauntingly difficult.

---

216. "Transatlantic Economic Council," United States Department of State, https://www.state.gov/p/eur/rt/eu/tec.

The other big challenge still awaits any attempt to strike a narrow deal with Europe. This can be thought of as "not missing the last train out of the station." To see this one, consider the position of an American farmer trying to get better access to the European market. Given a long-standing European reluctance to open its agricultural market to competition, the best opportunity would be likely to come in the context of a trade agreement, when access to the European market might be acquired in exchange for reciprocal European access to a politically sensitive American sector.

The problem the farmer would face is that the opportunities have been few and far between. After 1979 there was one round of GATT trade talks completed, the Uruguay Round. It was meant to liberalize agricultural trade, but made limited progress and largely set the stage for subsequent rounds. The subsequent Doha Round was never completed. Thus, over a span of almost 40 years, there have been almost no chances to exert leverage on Europe through a trade agreement to gain access.

Now imagine that a new, narrow trade agreement between the United States and the European Union were to appear. Suppose it is narrow enough that it excludes agriculture. The implication might be that the farmer should wait for the next opportunity to come along. But given the experience of recent decades, the farmer could be old by the time that happens. A more likely scenario is that the farmer, feeling a bit impatient, would lobby his senators to oppose any agreement that did not meet the needs of US agriculture. And with the opposition of US agriculture, it would be difficult to get a bill through the US Senate.

The idea of a quick, narrow agreement between the United States and the European Union is very appealing. However, given the difficulty of remaining issues and the political pressures for breadth, it would be very hard to pull off.

WTO

Given the earlier discussion about the economic and political efficiency of large trade agreements, the WTO would seem to be a natural place to try to reach new trade accords. Before it could play that role, however, the WTO has its own issues to overcome. When the WTO was created in the mid-1990s, there was some hope that it could function like a legislature, regularly producing new trade rules in a less cumbersome fashion than the traditional large rounds.

That hope went largely unrealized. After unsuccessful attempts to launch a new round, the WTO's centerpiece effort has been the Doha Development Agenda. Those talks have lasted for years and produced only fragments of what was first intended. The principal problem has been the inability to circumvent any major country that declared itself in opposition to a deal. With the WTO looking for consensus, any serious opposition meant impasse. The need to bring all members to consensus also meant that deals had to be sufficiently broad to allow for cross-cutting bargains.

To date, major countries of the trading world have responded to impasses at the WTO by pursuing regional trade agreements, such as TPP and TTIP. There is an alternative, however: the WTO could return to the practice of plurilateral agreements among a subset of its members. This had been standard practice under the GATT. If a critical mass of countries signed on to a deal, it could be viable.[217] The downside was that a patchwork of deals with differing memberships could be the result. The upside was that no single country had the ability to block all progress. Given the extent to which the WTO has been sidelined as a negotiating forum since Doha talks failed in the summer of 2008, it may be time to reconsider the devotion to purity and comprehensive participation.

Issues

What of the particular stances on trade that make up a modern US trade agreement? These were the issues discussed in the previous section. Once the appropriate forum in which to conduct talks is sorted out, are there any changes that could be made to the standard US approach to help heal the rifts that have afflicted US trade policy?

The challenge is not identifying traditional stances that could be reversed, but finding those for which a change prompts a net increase in support for trade agreements. The discussion below divides a selection of issues into three categories: a sparsely populated category of easy solutions, a more populous category of solutions that are difficult but worth trying, and finally, a well-populated set of changes that would likely serve as nonstarters.

---

217. This approach is sometimes referred to as "variable geometry." See Levy, "Do We Need an Undertaker for the Single Undertaking?"

Easy solutions

One clear, obvious change to the traditional US negotiating posture
in trade negotiations involves transparency. Critics have persistently
complained that trade negotiations are conducted in secret. This can
mean that important provisions that would change regulatory practice,
for example, may not be made available to public scrutiny until the
negotiations are complete. That leaves little practical room to push for
modification.

The rationale for secrecy is not hard to understand. For negotiations
to succeed, the negotiating leads must be able to explore ideas without being pilloried for any sensitive proposal they might consider. And,
to be fair, negotiations such as TPP proceeded with groups of cleared
advisors who were authorized to look at texts as they were being negotiated and to provide feedback. Such groups included those concerned
with such controversial issues as labor and the environment. The current advisory group on labor, for example, includes leaders of the AFL-
CIO, the Service Employees International Union, the Steelworkers, and
the Teamsters.[218]

There are two problems with the use of advisory groups, however.
The first is that they are just that—advisory. If the labor leaders dislike
a trade agreement presented to them, they can say so behind closed
doors, but their privileged access gives them no authority to block the
trade agreement. While it is certainly hard enough to make progress on
trade deals without introducing a new layer of veto players, the current
impotence of the advisory groups limits the extent to which the represented groups may feel their concerns have received a fair hearing.[219]

The second and bigger problem is the lack of trust in expertise that
characterizes modern policy discussions. Trump made this a core tenet
of his 2016 campaign, at one point saying, "The experts are terrible. . .
. Look at the mess we're in with all these experts that we have. Look at

---

218. "Labor Advisory Committee Members," Office of the United States Trade
     Representative, https://ustr.gov/about-us/advisory-committees/labor
     -advisory-committee-lac.
219. Kai Oppermann and Klaus Brummer, "Veto Player Approaches in Foreign
     Policy Analysis," *Oxford Research Encyclopedias* (August 2017),
     http://doi.org/10.1093/acrefore/9780190228637.013.386.

the mess."[220] To the extent this captures popular sentiment, the implication for trade policy is that allowing experts to have special access to trade negotiations is unlikely to satisfy public concerns.

The need, then, is for a middle ground between negotiations being held in public and the current, closely held approach. One possibility would be to enhance the role of Congress in the process. Executive branch trade negotiators are supposed to consult key congressional committees anyway. When there is a general sense of the types of proposals under discussion in trade agreements, Congress could hold hearings to gauge public and expert sentiment on the topics.

This would remain a balancing act. If those hearings present negotiators with multiple new red lines they cannot cross, this would make their jobs substantially harder. On the other hand, if public sentiment is such that those red lines exist and make it impossible to pass an agreement with the objectionable clauses, then it is better to know sooner than later.

Any negotiating administration will need to judge between the ultimata that need to be taken seriously and those that are really empty posturing.[221] To some extent, the more public approach advocated here is another way of saying that US administrations cannot take public support for agreements for granted and need to be making the public case more vociferously.

Difficult-but-worth-trying solutions

It would be nice if the list of easy solutions were longer, but after quickly exhausting the simple and viable solutions we come to those that are difficult but worth trying. Perhaps foremost on this list are programs to help workers who have been harmed by trade.

As discussed previously, trade has often been a scapegoat for ill effects that stem primarily from other causes such as technological change. This is the major challenge to creating such a program: how can we accurately identify those workers who truly are harmed by trade? This leads to a related question that has plagued such attempts: why do we care only about workers who are displaced by trade,

---

220. Nick Gass, "Trump: 'The Experts Are Terrible,'" *Politico*, April 4, 2016, https://www.politico.com/blogs/2016-gop-primary-live-updates-and -results/2016/04/donald-trump-foreign-policy-experts-221528.

221. For a good discussion of red lines in trade negotiations, see Dmitry Grozoubinksi, "50 Shades of Red Line," *Trade Explained*, September 9, 2018, https://www.explaintrade.com/blogs/2018/9/8/50-shades-of-red-line.

as opposed to those displaced by technological shifts or domestic competition?

There has been a long-standing attempt to link worker assistance to trade as a means to broaden support for trade agreements. A program administered by the Department of Labor (DOL), known as Trade Adjustment Assistance (TAA), attempts to cushion the blow of job dislocation due to trade.[222] The intent of TAA is to provide compensation and retraining assistance to workers in industries most affected by trade liberalization.

The mechanics are fairly simple: a company or its employees can petition the DOL for relief because of lost wages due to import competition or trade-related circumstances. If the DOL finds sufficient evidence that the job loss or reduction in hours is a result of foreign competition, the DOL provides workers with income support (supplemental to unemployment insurance), training allowances, and reimbursement for their job search and relocation fees. Those who qualify are allowed up to three years of benefits to cover living expenses, relocation, and schooling to retrain in an employable field.

An initial form of "adjustment assistance" was included in the 1962 Trade Expansion Act and was supported by the AFL-CIO, notwithstanding some reservations on the specifics.[223] In lieu of merely compensating affected workers with unemployment benefits to redistribute the gains from trade, the idea was that helping workers retrain for new positions would create both a more competitive US labor market and a more efficient economy.[224] Just over a decade later in the Trade Act of 1974, adjustment assistance was rebranded as TAA and bolstered by raising the available benefits and placing it under the DOL.[225]

In its approximately 50 years of existence, TAA has proven only marginally effective in accommodating workers from affected industries. Benefits can be slow-moving through state agencies, and although the DOL has certified 4.8 million workers since TAA's inception, only 2.2

---

222. "Trade Adjustment Assistance for Workers," United States Department of Labor, https://www.doleta.gov/tradeact.
223. Edward Alden, *Failure to Adjust: How Americans Got Left Behind in the Global Economy* (New York: Rowman and Littlefield, 2017), 111, 118.
224. Alden, *Failure to Adjust*, 112–13.
225. Alden, *Failure to Adjust*, 120. Placing it under the DOL as opposed to the Tariff Commission was meant to increase the number of accepted claims.

million have taken advantage of the job training assistance.[226] Moreover, DOL reports suggest that wages are lower for program participants who undergo retraining than for those who do not participate in the program at all, reducing the incentive for many to undergo retraining.[227]

Why do those who receive TAA retraining assistance not do better? The problem is stickier than it seems. First, many dislocated workers find the retraining regimen too difficult to complete. Many of those undergoing training often do not have the skills to prosper in school after years working in a specific field. Participants can be constrained by the types of jobs that are available. Gender biases may hinder many TAA recipients from training in new and growing fields such as education or nursing. Finally, geography becomes a sticking point. Even if jobs are available after retraining, openings may be in other regions of the country, which is particularly difficult for those with families or those who have negative equity in their homes.

The usefulness of the TAA programs as a means to build support for trade agreements has diminished over the past several decades. TAA suffered a rocky decade during the Reagan administration, being nearly eliminated on several occasions, only to be saved with a reduced budget.[228] By the time of the Clinton administration—as evidenced by the NAFTA Transitional Adjustment Assistance of 1994—TAA had become part of Congress' strategy to recertify TPA.

Similar expansions and extensions of TAA have been built into the recertification of TPA ever since, often to appease trade-skeptical members of Congress. During President Bush's request to reauthorize TPA in 2002, Congress enlarged the scope of benefits for those wishing to apply for TAA. As part of the American Recovery and Reinvestment Act of 2009, TAA was again enlarged and expanded to soften the blow of

---

226. In fact, recent studies have placed the net benefit to society of the current TAA program at nearly -$54,000 per participant. See Ronald D'Amico and Peter Z. Schochet, *The Evaluation of the Trade Adjustment Assistance Program: A Synthesis of Major Findings* (Social Policy Research Associates and Mathematica, 2012), 69, https://www.mathematica-mpr.com/download -media?MediaItemId=%7BDE128B8A-0456-41C0-96B0-ACB6D7752D1D %7D.

227. United States Department of Labor, *Report to the Committee on Finance of the Senate and the Committee on Ways and Means of the House of Representatives* (Washington, DC: United States Department of Labor, Employment and Training Administration, 2015), https://www.doleta.gov /tradeact/docs/AnnualReport15.pdf.

228. Alden, *Failure to Adjust*, 121.

nationwide layoffs. In 2009 and 2011 Congress again approved expansion of the TAA program, making it available for service-sector workers for the first time.

However, in 2015, when President Obama requested reauthorization of TPA to finalize TPP negotiations, the labor movement surprisingly moved against the TPA–TAA bill, sinking a bipartisan consensus that had developed over several decades.[229] Eventually passing in separate bills, the 2015 TPA renewal extricated TAA legislation completely, leaving the program intact only in stand-alone legislation.[230]

While there is a reasonably broad consensus that the United States should work to help those displaced by trade, the difficulty lies in identifying those people and figuring out an effective means of help. On the question of dealing with job loss and displacement, it is worth remembering that the US economy churns jobs at the rate of approximately 5 million separations and additions monthly, with only a fraction caused by international competition.[231]

One potential solution is to roll TAA into a broader assistance and job-training program that reflects the realities of a 21st-century economy by including it as part of a larger effort to retrain those in low-skilled labor sectors and struggling regions.[232] Some approaches such as facilitating worker savings for retraining would probably incur minimal costs. Broader programs that provide training and support would cost more. To give a rough idea, TAA spends approximately $9,600 per enrollee annually, with an average of 65,000 enrollees from 2013 to 2015.[233]

With a narrow or broad program, the fundamental challenge of how to help workers who are displaced in middle age will remain. Experience to date has provided some hints of how to do this effectively, but the problem remains an exceedingly difficult one. It is also unclear whether

229. Russell Berman, "A Big Win for Big Labor," *The Atlantic*, June 12, 2015, https://www.theatlantic.com/politics/archive/2015/06/a-big-win-for-big-labor/395699.

230. "H.R. 1295 (114th): Trade Preferences Extension Act of 2015" (data, GovTrack), https://www.govtrack.us/congress/bills/114/hr1295/summary.

231. "Job Openings and Labor Turnover Survey," Department of Labor, Bureau of Labor Statistics, https://www.bls.gov/jlt.

232. Grant Aldonas, Robert Lawrence, and Matthew Slaughter, *Succeeding in the Global Economy: An Adjustment Assistance Program for American Workers* (Washington, DC: The Financial Services Forum, July 2008), https://sites.hks.harvard.edu/fs/rlawrence/fsf_adjustment_assistance _plan.pdf.

233. United States Department of Labor, *Report to the Committee*.

affordable approaches would garner sufficient public support to break existing logjams over trade measures. That is particularly difficult to gauge, given the potential divergence between public beliefs about trade-induced job loss and the evidence.

A second, difficult topic that may be open to bipartisan solution involves protections for investors. As described in the previous section, both US and European trade agreements have made use of the ISDS system for decades. However, the ISDS clause was the basis of TPP objections in the United States and of large protests in Europe against TTIP.[234]

To consider alternatives, it is worth noting both what proponents hope to get from such investor protections and what opponents fear. The best-known group of proponents are multinational corporations, who are looking for protection against arbitrary loss of their investments abroad. Their fear is that a developing country could maliciously undermine or eliminate the value of their investments. A less prominent but no less important constituency for ISDS is the group of developing countries that has sought to sign such agreements. These governments are often trying to overcome shaky economic track records and see trade agreements as a way to commit credibly to a more responsible economic path and thereby attract a quick influx of foreign investment.[235]

The key concerns for critics are the possibility that ISDS can be used to block regulatory policy changes and that it provides undue power to multinational corporations. On the regulatory point, the worry is that a desirable piece of domestic environmental regulation, for example, might saddle a poor developing country with a sufficiently large liability to a foreign investor that the country forgoes adopting the regulation. On the undue power critique, critics note that ISDS is a rare instance in which private actors get access to such dispute settlement, normally reserved for state-to-state dealings. They ask why only investors should have such a right.

---

234. Elizabeth Warren, "The Trans-Pacific Partnership Clause Everyone Should Oppose," *The Washington Post*, February 25, 2015, https://www.washingtonpost.com/opinions/kill-the-dispute-settlement -language-in-the-trans-pacific-partnership/2015/02/25/ec7705a2-bd1e -11e4-b274-e5209a3bc9a9_story.html?utm_term=.6e3576fb9ed2.

235. Phil Levy, "The United States-Peru Trade Promotion Agreement: What Did You Expect?" *SSRN* (November 6, 2009), http://dx.doi.org/10.2139/ssrn .1501243.

The international legal analyst Simon Lester provides an analysis that suggests dimensions along which an acceptable compromise might be found. The possibilities raised by his work include the following.[236]

One could create a domestic mechanism to launch state-to-state investment disputes of the sort that currently exists in the United States in Section 301 of the Trade Act of 1974. This would address the critique that the investor role deviates from standard international law and excessively empowers multinational corporations.

One could be more explicit about which sort of regulations could be seen as capricious and actionable and which could be exempted. This could be similar to other trade arguments about whether regulatory measures are necessary to protect the public or are simply disguised protectionism. Such arguments often try to set a standard such as scientific evidence backing up a concern. This could lessen concerns that investor protections undermine important regulatory goals.

There has been an awkwardness about offering ISDS as a way to circumvent domestic legal processes even in countries with reputable court systems such as the United States and Canada. Given the trenchant criticisms, one could explore applying ISDS only to legal systems that fell below some international standard. Passing explicit judgment on foreign legal systems in this way, however, could be a politically fraught exercise.

Reworking such legal standards is anything but easy, particularly as countries have worked existing standards into their agreements and those standards have gained powerful constituencies. The European Union, in an attempt to address ISDS criticisms, put forward the idea of a "Multilateral Investment Court."[237] That proposal has, to date, drawn little support from the United States.

In both the cases of TAA and ISDS, there seem to be sufficient common objectives of proponents and opponents that compromise might be reached, though the challenges are substantial.

---

236. Simon Lester, "The ISDS Controversy: How We Got Here and Where Next," CATO Institute, July 1, 2016, https://www.cato.org/publications /commentary/isds-controversy-how-we-got-here-where-next. While the underlying legal analysis is Lester's, he does not bear any responsibility for these specific proposals.
237. European Commission, *A Multilateral Investment Court: State of the Union 2017* (Brussels: European Commission, September 2017), http://trade .ec.europa.eu/doclib/docs/2017/september/tradoc_156042.pdf.

Nonstarters

There are several prominent topics on which it is highly unlikely
that modifications to trade agreements will be able to address critics' concerns.

> ▶ **Bilateral trade deficits:** As described above, the trade deficit
> usually expands or contracts in response to macroeconomic
> factors, not trade policy. While a country like South Korea might
> temporarily manipulate its bilateral balance with the United States
> by switching its purchases from another country to a US source,
> even that does not provide any lasting guarantee of a targeted
> bilateral balance. There are three fatal objections to including
> bilateral trade deficits as an objective of trade agreements. First,
> no economic benefit comes from doing so. Second, no policy
> measures can readily meet the objective. Third, the attempt to
> meet the objective would require *greater* government involve-
> ment in manipulating trade, the opposite of the standard push for
> open markets and a level playing field.

> ▶ **Minimum wage requirements:** Given popular concerns about US
> manufacturing being undercut by offshoring to take advantage of
> low-cost labor abroad, the idea of setting a minimum wage has
> seemed appealing. The problem is twofold. First, productivity var-
> ies substantially between countries. In the United States in 2016,
> for example, output averaged roughly $69.90 per hour worked. In
> Mexico, the OECD estimates the comparable figure at $20.90.[238]
> A set wage that did not take productivity into account could be
> economically disastrous if set too high.[239] Second, even if Mexico
> or another developing country was to set a relatively high min-
> imum wage, there would be serious concerns among congres-
> sional Republicans in the United States about embracing such a
> restrictive labor market policy.

---

238. Organisation for Economic Co-operation and Development, "Level of GDP
Per Capita and Productivity" (data), https://stats.oecd.org/viewhtml.aspx
?datasetcode=PDB_LV&lang=en.

239. Note first that these numbers are overall output per worker hour, not marginal worker productivities. Further, even strong minimum wage advocates
in the United States do not advocate for a $50/hour minimum wage. Given
the productivity ratios, that would be the rough equivalent of a $15/hour
minimum wage in Mexico.

▶ **Currency manipulation:** Exchange rates move in response to the relative demand for goods and services trade but also in response to the relative demand for investments. Thus, an exceedingly common reason for a currency to drop is that a country's central bank drops its interest rates, thus making its bonds less attractive and inducing money to flow out. The problem with including tough currency manipulation language in trade agreements is that, if it is to bind, it will have to limit the ability of central banks to cut interest rates. Yet that ability is at the core of monetary policy. In the United States, for example, the central bank is independent in its operation and tasked with targeting price stability and full employment. For the same reason the United States would be unwilling to have its hands tied in the event of an economic downturn, other countries are unlikely to accept such provisions in trade agreements.

This is not to say that such topics will never appear in a trade agreement. Mexico, for example, has indicated some openness to including currency manipulation language in the revised NAFTA, and the tentative agreement also includes some *de facto* minimum wage requirements.[240] The question is whether such innovation survives the policy adoption process in anything more than symbolic form.

Conclusion

There would be a substantial benefit to overcoming the bipartisan rifts that have hampered the creation of trade policy for the last 25 years. The narrow, partisan approach to trade has resulted in slim majorities that empower each marginal interest group in its demands. Meanwhile, each major deal in recent years, from NAFTA to the Uruguay Round, to the Doha Round, to the Colombia, Korea, and TPP trade agreements, have all stretched from an administration of one party to the administration of the other party. It has proven increasingly difficult to make

---

240. Anthony Esposito, "Mexico Open to NAFTA Accord Against Forest Manipulation -Minister," Reuters, October 24, 2017, https://www.reuters .com/article/uk-trade-nafta-mexico/mexico-open-to-nafta-accord-against-forex-manipulation-minister-idUSKBN1CU03Y; Claude Barfield, "$15 an Hour for Mexican Workers? 'Export Protectionism' Lives!" *AEIdeas* (blog), American Enterprise Institute, April 5, 2018, http://www.aei .org/publication/15-an-hour-for-mexican-workers-export-protectionism -lives.

international economic policy for the benefit of the American people in the absence of a more bipartisan consensus.

This chapter provided an illustrative—not exhaustive—list of some changes that might facilitate such a consensus. There was the rare issue that was relatively easy—greater transparency in trade negotiation. There were challenging issues where there appears to be some real hope of compromise such as trade adjustment assistance and investor protections. Then there were issues that play to popular fears but are unlikely to play any role in sensible economic policy.

So what can be done about this final group? Of course, if a critic's true goal is to block a policy, then such "poison pills" hold a special appeal. They either provide a pretext for rejecting an agreement, or they render the agreement undesirable if adopted. It is worth acknowledging that in some such cases the only remedy will be education—the purpose of this monograph.

Chapter V: Conclusion

What if the United States does not find a way to restore bipartisan support for an engaged international trade policy? What if the Trump administration continues on its course of unilateral erection of trade barriers coupled with unorthodox, abrasive, and haphazard negotiations?

At the time of this writing, there was substantial optimism about the Trump approach. To somewhat of a surprise, the Trump administration managed to conclude NAFTA renegotiation talks by an October 1, 2018, deadline. Perhaps, some thought, this pointed to a new way forward.

Yet the Trump administration's NAFTA approach hinged on increasing rather than decreasing barriers to trade.[241] It is not at all clear that the agreement will get through Congress within the next year. If it does, it would be the fastest passage of a US trade agreement since the Peru agreement in 2007.

In late 2018 the White House did notify Congress of its intention to negotiate agreements with Japan, Europe, and a post-Brexit United Kingdom. The negotiations have been very slow to start, however, and given the lags in the process, it is unlikely that any will be negotiated and passed by the end of Trump's term in 2021. There are also no active multilateral talks under way at the WTO.

One of the striking differences between the trade wars of the 1930s and the trade wars of 2018 was that in the latter the United States basically stood alone. Whereas earlier, many nations had been raising trade barriers and cutting themselves off from the rest of the world. This time it was just the Trump administration. The European Union was signing trade deals, separately, with Canada and Japan. The nations of the Asia-Pacific region were in discussions to implement TPP and conclude an additional agreement, the Regional Comprehensive Economic Partnership, which includes China. Both the Asian agreements excluded the United States.

There are several important implications of the sidelining of the United States in trade. First, the United States loses its strong voice

---

241. Phil Levy, "Trump Faces a Car Conundrum on NAFTA Deal," *Forbes*, October 5, 2018, https://www.forbes.com/sites/phillevy/2018/10/05 /trump-trade-master-plan-meets-car-conundrum/#5268065edbeb.

in setting rules and standards. As described above, these can be as important as tariffs for determining whether US companies have access to foreign markets. In yielding to other countries on setting standards, US companies could be saddled with costly transitions or excluded from global competitions.

A second important cost would come with the extrication of the United States from global supply chains, a stated objective of key members of the Trump administration.[242] Given that other countries will still have access to global supply chains, this is the equivalent of a single construction company swearing off the use of power tools so as to increase the demand for labor. Such a company would very soon cease to be competitive.

The competitiveness of countries is not directly comparable to the competitiveness of companies. Companies go out of business, while countries do not. But there is ample experience with what happens when countries become costly and risky places to do business. Capital and mobile labor will flow where the returns are highest. The United States is far too important an economy for investors to abandon it altogether, but even a limited pullback could have lasting and painful consequences for American well-being.

A final cost lies beyond the realm of economics. US global economic engagement has long been intertwined with its security alliances. This was true when the United States sought to bolster Western European economies against communism in the wake of World War II. It was true when the United States worked to prevent crime and terrorism from emanating out of economically failed states. It was true when the United States used trade deals to solidify its role in the Asia-Pacific region.

It is not plausible that the United States can be abrasive and unreliable in its international economic dealings, yet still be considered steadfast as a security partner. If the United States was willing to walk away from South Korea over steel trade, for example, how confident would the South Koreans be that the United States would stand firm in the face of a North Korean attack?

This was the state of the world in late 2018. The United States continued to trade with the rest of the world, but barriers were rising quickly. The United States was perceived to be belligerent and self-absorbed.

---

242. Shawn Donnan, "US Trade Chief Seeks to Reshore Supply Chain," *Financial Times*, January 31, 2017, https://www.ft.com/content/8dc63502 -e7c7-11e6-893c-082c54a7f539.

The only countries that engaged in formal trade talks were those that did so under duress—South Korea, Canada, and Mexico. Others attempted to avoid trade breakdowns while distancing themselves.

The promises of protectionist benefits were as illusory in 2018 as in the 1930s. Farmers suffered from lower crop prices as their exports were blocked by retaliatory trade barriers. Manufacturers faced higher prices for imported parts. And the trade deficit continued to grow.

These were the short-term costs. The more serious, long-term penalties are still to come.

Yet they are not inevitable. US credibility in trade has been undeniably damaged but perhaps not yet beyond repair. Public support for trade has grown, stirred by the recent trade conflicts and evidence of the damage they can do. There is room for compromise between parties and innovation in trade policy. It was notable that bills to block national security tariffs were introduced in both the Senate and the House with bipartisan sponsorship.

The path to a new trade consensus will not be easy. The economic complaints of those lamenting the loss of manufacturing jobs are real. There are strong political temptations to engage in demagoguery. There are also strong forces pushing to constrain trade policy choices.

The potential gains to restoring a trade consensus are both large and increasingly evident. A first step toward reaching a viable solution is to better understand the problem and the choices available. That has been the purpose of this work.

Acknowledgments

I would like to express my gratitude to the Charles Koch Foundation for its generous support, which made this monograph possible. I benefited greatly from the insights of a bipartisan group of trade experts who shared their insights at a full-day event at the Chicago Council on Global Affairs in the fall of 2016. I appreciated the wise counsel of the Chicago Council's Vice President for Studies, Brian Hanson, as well as the invaluable assistance of my Research Associate, Alex Hitch. I was and remain grateful for the patient support of Veronique Barrotteaux throughout the writing process.

About the author

Phil Levy received his AB in economics from the University of Michigan and his PhD in economics from Stanford University. He has published analytical works in journals such as *The American Economic Review* and *The Journal of International Economics*. His government work included two stints at the Council of Economic Advisors in the White Houses of the first and second Presidents Bush, the latter of which was as Senior Economist for Trade. He also served as a member of Secretary of State Rice's Policy Planning Staff. He has taught at Yale University's Department of Economics, the University of Virginia's Darden School of Business, and Georgetown University's McDonough School of Business. He currently teaches international business strategy at Northwestern University's Kellogg School of Management. He is Senior Fellow on the Global Economy at the Chicago Council on Global Affairs, advises government officials and legislators, and writes regularly for publications such as *Forbes* and *The Hill*.

Reference List

Agama, Laurie-Ann, and Christine A. McDaniel. "The NAFTA Preference and U.S.-Mexico Trade." Working paper No. 2002-10-A, Office of Economics, United States International Trade Commission, Washington, DC, October 2002. https://www.usitc.gov/publications/332/ec200210a.pdf.

Alden, Edward. *Failure to Adjust: How Americans Got Left Behind in the Global Economy*. New York: Rowman and Littlefield, 2017.

Aldonas, Grant, Robert Lawrence, and Matthew Slaughter. *Succeeding in the Global Economy: An Adjustment Assistance Program for American Workers*. Washington, DC: The Financial Services Forum, July 2008. https://sites.hks.harvard.edu/fs/rlawrence/fsf_adjustment_assistance_plan.pdf.

Alire, David, and Michael O'Boyle. "The Rocky History of NAFTA." Reuters, September 1, 2017. https://www.reuters.com/article/us-trade-nafta-timeline/the-rocky-history-of-nafta-idUSKCN1BC5IL?il=0.

An, David. "Critical Rare Earths, National Security, and U.S.-China Interactions." PhD diss., Pardee RAND Graduate School, 2014. https://www.rand.org/pubs/rgs_dissertations/RGSD337.html.

Autor, David H., David Dorn, and Gordon H. Hanson. "The China Syndrome: Local Labor Market Effects of Import Competition in the United States." *American Economic Review* 103, no. 6 (October 2013): 2121–68. https://www.aeaweb.org/articles?id=10.1257/aer.103.6.2121.

Bach, Natasha. "Don't Use Huawei Phones, Warn 6 Top U.S. Intelligence Chiefs." *Fortune*, February 14, 2018. http://fortune.com/2018/02/14/intelligence-chiefs-warn-against-using-huawei-phones.

Barfield, Claude. "$15 an Hour for Mexican Workers? 'Export Protectionism' Lives!" *AEIdeas* (blog), American Enterprise Institute, April 5, 2018. http://www.aei.org/publication/15-an-hour-for-mexican-workers-export-protectionism-lives.

Barfield, Claude, and Philip Levy. "Tales of the South Pacific: President Obama and the Transpacific Partnership." Washington, DC: American Enterprise Institute for Public Policy Research, 2009. http://www.aei.org/wp-content/uploads/2011/10/09-IEO-Dec-g.pdf.

Basile, Caroline. "NAHB: Lumber Tariffs Increasing Cost of Homebuilding." *Housingwire*, June 14, 2018. https://www.housingwire.com/articles/43690-nahb-lumber-tariffs-increasing-cost-of-homebuilding.

Berman, Russell. "A Big Win for Big Labor." *The Atlantic*, June 12, 2015. https://www.theatlantic.com/politics/archive/2015/06/a-big-win-for-big-labor/395699.

Blonigen, Bruce A., and Thomas J. Prusa. "Dumping and Antidumping Duties." Working paper 21573, NBER, 2015.

Boffey, Daniel, and Jessica Elgot. "Brussels Attacks Liam Fox's 'Ignorant' Remarks on Chlorinated Chicken." *The Guardian*, July 25, 2017. https://www.theguardian.com/politics/2017/jul/25/brussels-attacks-liam-foxs-ignorant-remarks-chlorinated-chicken-eu-trade-deal-us.

Bolton, Alexander. "Senate Approves Fast-Track, Sending Trade Bill to White House." *The Hill*, June 24, 2015. http://thehill.com/homenews/senate/246035-senate-approves-fast-track-sending-trade-bill-to-white-house.

Bowden, John. "Trump Defends Tariffs: When We Use Them 'Foolish People Scream!'" *The Hill*, August 4, 2018. https://thehill.com/policy/finance/trade/400404-trump-defends-tariffs-when-we-use-them-foolish-people-scream.

Bown, Chad. "Sweating the Auto Details of Trump's Trade Deal with Mexico." *Trade & Investment Policy Watch* (blog). Washington, DC: Peterson Institute for International Economics, August 29, 2018. https://piie.com/blogs/trade-investment-policy-watch/sweating-auto-details-trumps-trade-deal-mexico.

———. "Trump's Steel and Aluminum Tariffs Are Counterproductive. Here Are 5 More Things You Need to Know." *Trade & Investment Policy Watch* (blog). Washington, DC: Peterson Institute for International Economics, March 7, 2018. https://piie.com/blogs/trade-investment-policy-watch/trumps-steel-and-aluminum-tariffs-are-counterproductive-here-are.

Brandt, Loren, Debin Ma, and Thomas G. Rawski. "From Divergence to Convergence: Reevaluating the History Behind China's Economic Boom." *Journal of Economic Literature* 52, no. 1 (2014): 45–123. http://doi.org/10.1257/jel.52.1.45.

Caliendo, Lorenzo, and Fernando Parro. "Estimates of the Trade and Welfare Effects of NAFTA." NBER Working Paper No. 1850, *Review of Economic Studies* 82, no. 1 (2015): 1–44. http://doi.org/10.3386/w18508.

Caporal, Jack, and William Reinsch. "From NAFTA to USMCA: What's New and What's Next?" Washington, DC: Center for Strategic and International Studies, October 3, 2018. https://www.csis.org/analysis/nafta-usmca-whats-new-and-whats-next.

Carroll, Rory. "'So Far from God, So Close to the US': Mexico's Troubled Past with Its Neighbor." *The Guardian*, February 1, 2017. https://www.theguardian.com/us-news/2017/feb/01/donald-trump-us-mexico-relations-history.

Chen, Yawen, and Karl Plume. "China Customs Expands Checks on U.S. Fruit Imports: Sources." Reuters, May 3, 2018. https://www.reuters.com/article/us-usa-trade-china-fruits/chinese-customs-expands-checks-on-u-s-fruit-imports-sources-idUSKBN1I428K.

"China 1980." PopulationPyramid.net. https://www.populationpyramid.net/china/1980.

"China Takes on the EU at the WTO." *The Economist*, December 7, 2017. https://www.economist.com/finance-and-economics/2017/12/07/china-takes-on-the-eu-at-the-wto.

China's Exchange Rate Policy: Hearing Before the Committee on Ways and Means, U.S. House of Representatives, 111th Cong., 2nd Sess. Statement of Philip I. Levy, PhD, Resident Scholar, The American Enterprise Institute, March 24, 2010. https://www.govinfo.gov/content/pkg/CHRG-111hhrg63077/pdf/CHRG-111hhrg63077.pdf.

"China's Reported Offer to Slash Trade Deficit with US Is About Politics: Economist." CNBC, May 18, 2018. https://www.cnbc.com/2018/05/18/us-china-trade-chinas-offer-is-more-politics-than-economics.html.

Cho, Sungjoon. "The Bush Administration and Democrats Reach a Bipartisan Deal on Trade Policy." *American Society of International Law* 11, no. 15 (May 31, 2007). https://www.asil.org/insights/volume/11/issue/15/bush-administration-and-democrats-reach-bipartisan-deal-trade-policy.

"Ck6432 High Precision Small Flat Bed Horizontal Metal CNC Lathe." *Focus Technology*. https://lycncmachine.en.made-in-china.com/product/fKNEYzPAOLUF/China-Ck6432-High-Precision-Small-Flat-Bed-Horizontal-Metal-CNC-Lathe.html.

"Clinton and China: How Promise Self-Destructed." *The New York Times*, May 29, 1994. https://www.nytimes.com/1994/05/29/world/clinton-and-china-how-promise-self-destructed.html.

Cooper, William H. *The Jackson-Vanik Amendment and Candidate Countries for WTO Accession: Issues for Congress*. Washington, DC: Congressional Research Service, July 26, 2012. https://fas.org/sgp/crs/row/RS22398.pdf.

Congressional Record 1368. Daily edition, January 10, 1930. Statement of Sen. Reed Smoot. Quoted in Douglas A. Irwin. *Clashing over Commerce: A History of US Trade Policy*. Chicago: The University of Chicago Press, 2017.

Cox, Lydia, and Kadee Russ. "Will Steel Tariffs Put U.S. Jobs at Risk?" *Econofact*, February 26, 2018. https://econofact.org/will-steel-tariffs-put-u-s-jobs-at-risk.

D'Amico, Ronald, and Peter Z. Schochet. *The Evaluation of the Trade Adjustment Assistance Program: A Synthesis of Major Findings.* Social Policy Research Associates and Mathematica, 2012. https://www.mathematica-mpr.com/download-media?MediaItemId =%7BDE128B8A-0456-41C0-96B0-ACB6D7752D1D%7D.

Deaton, Jamie Page. "What the Disaster in Japan Means for Car Buyers Here." U.S. News and World Report, March 29, 2011. https://cars .usnews.com/cars-trucks/what-the-disaster-in-japan-means-for-car -buyers-here.

Denning, Dorothy. "Cyberwar: How Chinese Hackers Became a Major Threat to the U.S." *Newsweek*, October 5, 2017. https://www .newsweek.com/chinese-hackers-cyberwar-us-cybersecurity -threat-678378.

Destler, I. M. "America's Uneasy History with Free Trade." *Harvard Business Review*, April 28, 2016. https://hbr.org/2016/04/americas -uneasy-history-with-free-trade.

Donnan, Shawn. "US Trade Chief Seeks to Reshore Supply Chain." *Financial Times*, January 31, 2017. https://www.ft.com/content /8dc63502-e7c7-11e6-893c-082c54a7f539.

Eberstadt, Nicholas. "The Demographic Future: What Population Growth—and Decline—Means for the Global Economy." *Foreign Affairs* 89, no. 6 (2010): 54–64. http://www.jstor.org/stable/20788716.

Eilperin, Juliet. "House Defeats Fast-Track Trade Authority." *The Washington Post*, September 26, 1998. https://www.washingtonpost.com/wp -srv/politics/special/trade/stories/fasttrack092698.htm?noredirect=on.

Esposito, Anthony. "Mexico Open to NAFTA Accord Against Forest Manipulation -Minister." Reuters, October 24, 2017. https://www.reuters .com/article/uk-trade-nafta-mexico/mexico-open-to-nafta-accord -against-forex-manipulation-minister-idUSKBN1CU03Y.

European Commission. *A Multilateral Investment Court: State of the Union 2017*. Brussels: European Commission, September 2017. http://trade.ec.europa.eu/doclib/docs/2017/september/tradoc _156042.pdf.

———. "Cumulations." http://trade.ec.europa.eu/tradehelp/cumulation.

———. "What is Zeroing?" Press release. European Commission, February 6, 2012. http://europa.eu/rapid/press-release_MEMO-12-73_en.htm.

Farley, Robert. "Trump on the Stump." FactCheck.org, September 28, 2016. https://www.factcheck.org/2016/09/trump-on-the-stump.

Farnsworth, Clyde. "Reagan Acts to Restrict Machine Tool Imports." *The New York Times*, May 21, 1986. https://www.nytimes.com/1986 /05/21/business/reagan-acts-to-restrict-machine-tool-imports.html.

Federal Reserve Bank of New York. "Balance of Payments."
    https://www.newyorkfed.org/aboutthefed/fedpoint/fed40.html.

Finger, Michael J. "Implementing the Uruguay Round Agreements: Prob-
    lems for Developing Countries." *The World Economy* 24, no. 9 (Sep-
    tember 2001): 1097–108. https://doi.org/10.1111/1467-9701.00402.

Fish, Isaac Stone. "Trump's China-Bashing Id." *Slate*, December 22, 2016.
    https://slate.com/news-and-politics/2016/12/peter-navarro-trumps
    -trade-czar-embodies-the-china-bashing-id-of-his-campaign.html.

Fountain, Nick. "632: The Chicken Tax." Produced by Frances Harlow.
    Planet Money, NPR, January 25, 2017. Podcast, MP3 audio, 16:56.
    https://www.npr.org/templates/transcript/transcript.php?storyId
    =511663527.

Freund, Caroline. "Streamlining Rules of Origin in NAFTA." Policy brief.
    Washington, DC: Peterson Institute for International Economics,
    June 2017. https://piie.com/publications/policy-briefs/streamlining
    -rules-origin-nafta.

"From the GATT to the WTO: A Brief Overview." Research guide. Wash-
    ington, DC: Georgetown Law Library. Last modified September 25,
    2018. http://guides.ll.georgetown.edu/c.php?g=363556&p=4108235.

Gass, Nick. "Trump: 'The Experts Are Terrible.'" *Politico*, April 4, 2016.
    https://www.politico.com/blogs/2016-gop-primary-live-updates-and
    -results/2016/04/donald-trump-foreign-policy-experts-221528.

Gertler, Jeffrey. *What China's WTO Accession Is All About*. Washing-
    ton, DC: The World Bank, December 14, 2002. http://siteresources.
    worldbank.org/INTRANETTRADE/Resources/Gertler.pdf.

Gertz, Geoffrey. "What Will Trump's Embrace of Bilateralism Mean for
    America's Trade Partners?" The Brookings Institute, February 8,
    2017. https://www.brookings.edu/blog/future-development/2017/02
    /08/what-will-trumps-embrace-of-bilateralism-mean-for-americas
    -trade-partners.

Goldberg, Jonah. "Free Speech – Sometimes." *Townhall*, March 1, 2006.
    https://townhall.com/columnists/jonahgoldberg/2006/03/01/free
    -speech---sometimes-n1407826.

Government of Canada. "Consolidated TPP Text – Chapter 19 – Labour."
    Last modified December 6, 2016. https://international.gc.ca/trade
    -commerce/trade-agreements-accords-commerciaux/agr-acc/tpp
    -ptp/text-texte/19.aspx?lang=eng.

———. "Timeline of the CPTPP." Last modified December 17, 2018.
    https://international.gc.ca/trade-commerce/trade-agreements
    -accords-commerciaux/agr-acc/cptpp-ptpgp/timeline_negotiations
    -chronologie_negociations.aspx?lang=eng.

Gramer, Robbie. "Infographic: Here's How the Global GDP Is Divvied Up." *Foreign Policy*, February 24, 2017. https://foreignpolicy.com/2017/02/24/infographic-heres-how-the-global-gdp-is-divvied-up.

Gresser, Edward. "Taxing the Poor." *Foreign Affairs*, July 30, 2008. https://www.foreignaffairs.com/articles/united-states/2008-07-30/taxing-poor.

Grozoubinksi, Dmitry. "50 Shades of Red Line." *Trade Explained*, September 9, 2018. https://www.explaintrade.com/blogs/2018/9/8/50-shades-of-red-line.

Gruenberg, Mark. "Union Leaders to Trump: 'New NAFTA' Must Boost Workers' Rights, Wages." *People's World*, February 22, 2018. http://www.peoplesworld.org/article/union-leaders-to-trump-new-nafta-must-boost-workers-rights-wages.

Hee-Chul, Moon, and Choi Hyung-Jo. "FTA Revisions Lets U.S. Bypass Korean Regulations." *Korean Joongang Daily*, April 11, 2018. http://koreajoongangdaily.joins.com/news/article/article.aspx?aid=3046761.

Hicks, Michael, and Srikant Devaraj. *The Myth and the Reality of Manufacturing in America*. Muncie, IN: Ball State University, June 2015 and April 2017. https://conexus.cberdata.org/files/MfgReality.pdf.

Ho, Catherine. "Industry, Labor and Environmental Groups Gear Up to Oppose TPP Trade Deal." *The Washington Post*, October 6, 2015. https://www.washingtonpost.com/news/powerpost/wp/2015/10/06/industry-labor-and-environmental-groups-gear-up-to-oppose-tpp-trade-deal/?utm_term=.04f728ac582a.

Hoffman, David, and Erik Lundh. "'Huge' Trade Deficits Are Smaller Than You Think." *Bloomberg*, March, 18, 2018. https://www.bloomberg.com/view/articles/2018-03-18/big-u-s-china-trade-deficit-is-smaller-than-it-appears.

Hornbeck, J. F., and William H. Cooper. *Trade Promotion Authority and the Role of Congress in Trade Policy*. Washington, DC: Congressional Research Service, April 7, 2011. http://www.au.af.mil/au/awc/awcgate/crs/rl33743.pdf.

"H.R. 1295 (114th): Trade Preferences Extension Act of 2015." Data. GovTrack. https://www.govtrack.us/congress/bills/114/hr1295/summary.

"H.R. 2146: Defending Public Safety Employees' Retirement Act." Data. GovTrack. https://www.govtrack.us/congress/votes/114-2015/h374.

"H.R. 3005 (107th): Bipartisan Trade Promotion Authority Act of 2002." Data, GovTrack. https://www.govtrack.us/congress/votes/107-2001/h481.

Hsieh, Chang-Tai, and Peter J. Klenow. "Misallocation and Manufacturing TFP in China and India." *The Quarterly Journal of Economics* 124, no. 4 (2009): 1403–48.

Hufbauer, Gary. "Ross Perot Was Wrong About Nafta." *The New York Times*, November 25, 2013. https://www.nytimes.com /roomfordebate/2013/11/24/what-weve-learned-from-nafta/ross -perot-was-wrong-about-nafta.

Hufbauer, Gary, and Paul Grieco. "The Payoff from Globalization." Op-ed. Washington, DC: Peterson Institute for International Economics, June 7, 2005. https://piie.com/commentary/op-eds/payoff -globalization.

Irwin, Douglas A. *Clashing over Commerce: A History of US Trade Policy*. Chicago: The University of Chicago Press, 2017.

"Japan to Resist Bilateral Trade Deal with US and Push for TPP." *The Straits Times*, July 24, 2018. https://www.straitstimes.com/asia/east -asia/japan-to-resist-bilateral-trade-deal-with-us-and-push-for-tpp.

Johnson, Donald B., and Kirk H. Porter. *National Party Platforms, 1840-1972*. 5th ed. Urbana: University of Illinois Press, 1973. Quoted in Douglas A. Irwin. *Clashing over Commerce: A History of US Trade Policy*. Chicago: The University of Chicago Press, 2017.

Johnson, Renée. *U.S.-EU Poultry Dispute on the Use of Pathogen Reduction Treatments (PRTs)*. Washington, DC: Congressional Research Service, 2014. http://nationalaglawcenter.org/wp-content /uploads/assets/crs/R40199.pdf.

Josling, Tim, and Stefan Tangermann. "TTIP and Agriculture: Another Transatlantic Chicken War?" *Choices* 31, no. 2 (2016): 1–7. https:// ageconsearch.umn.edu/bitstream/235003/2/cmsarticle_501.pdf.

Kaika, Dimitra, and Efthimios Zervas. "The Environmental Kuznets Curve (EKC) Theory—Part A: Concept, Causes and the CO2 Emissions Case." *ScienceDirect* 62 (November 2013): 1392–402. https://doi .org/10.1016/j.enpol.2013.07.131.

Knoll, David D. "Section 232 of the Trade Expansion Act of 1962: Industrial Fasteners, Machine Tools and Beyond." *Maryland Journal of International Law* 10, no. 1 (1986). http://digitalcommons.law .umaryland.edu/mjil/vol10/iss1/4.

Krishna, Kala, and Anne Krueger. "Implementing Free Trade Areas: Rules of Origin and Hidden Protection." Working paper, International Trade and Investment, The National Bureau of Economic Research, January 1995. http://www.nber.org/papers/w4983.

Krober, Arthur. "Xi Jinping's Ambitious Agenda for Economic Reform in China." The Brookings Institute, November 17, 2013. https://www.brookings.edu/opinions/xi-jinpings-ambitious-agenda-for-economic-reform-in-china.

Lawder, David. "U.S. Commerce Dept Probing Steel 'Profiteering' After Tariffs." Reuters, June 20, 2018. https://www.reuters.com/article/us-usa-trade-steel/u-s-commerce-dept-probing-steel-profiteering-after-tariffs-idUSKBN1JG22W.

Lester, Simon. "The ISDS Controversy: How We Got Here and Where Next." CATO Institute, July 1, 2016. https://www.cato.org/publications/commentary/isds-controversy-how-we-got-here-where-next.

Levy, Philip. "Did China Trade Cost the United States 2.4 Million Jobs?" *Foreign Policy*, May 8, 2016. https://foreignpolicy.com/2016/05/08/did-china-trade-cost-the-united-states-2-4-million-jobs.

———. "Did Obama's Trade Agenda Just Quietly Run Out of Time?" *Foreign Policy*, August 3, 2015. https://foreignpolicy.com/2015/08/03/did-obamas-trade-agenda-just-quietly-run-out-of-time.

———. "Do We Need an Undertaker for the Single Undertaking? Considering the Angles of Variable Geometry." In *Economic Development & Multilateral Trade Cooperation*, edited by Simon J. Evenett and Bernard M. Hoekman, 419–37. Washington, DC: The World Bank; New York: Palgrave MacMillan, 2006.

———. "Doing a Job on NAFTA." Washington, DC: American Enterprise Institute, March 7, 2008. http://www.aei.org/publication/doing-a-job-on-nafta.

———. "Et Tu, Autos? The Case for National Security Tariffs Is Weak." *Forbes*, May 24, 2018. https://www.forbes.com/sites/phillevy/2018/05/24/et-tu-autos-more-national-security-tariffs/#167ebb1b59b4.

———. "Everything You Need to Know About the Long, Complex Process of Passing the TPA." *Foreign Policy*, June 18, 2015. https://foreignpolicy.com/2015/06/18/everything-you-need-to-know-about-the-impending-death-of-obamas-free-trade-dreams.

———. "The Commerce Department Makes a Feeble National Security Plea for Steel Protection." *Forbes*, February 16, 2018. https://www.forbes.com/sites/phillevy/2018/02/16/the-commerce-departments-feeble-national-security-plea-for-steel-protection/#4abe5bad42dc.

———. "The German Art of the Deal." *Forbes*, March 18, 2017. https://www.forbes.com/sites/phillevy/2017/03/18/the-german-art-of-the-deal/#492388c3225f.

———. "The TPP Train Could Still Get Derailed." *Foreign Policy*, January 6, 2016. https://foreignpolicy.com/2016/01/06/tpp-could-still-get -derailed-us-congress.

———. "The Treatment of Chinese SOEs in China's WTO Protocol of Accession." Working paper RSCAS 2017/04, Robert Schuman Centre for Advanced Studies, European University Institute. http://cadmus .eui.eu/bitstream/handle/1814/45984/RSCAS_2017_04.pdf ?sequence=1&isAllowed=y.

———. "The United States-Peru Trade Promotion Agreement: What Did You Expect?" *SSRN* (November 6, 2009). http://dx.doi.org/10.2139 /ssrn.1501243.

———. "Trump Faces a Car Conundrum on NAFTA Deal." *Forbes*, October 5, 2018. https://www.forbes.com/sites/phillevy/2018/10/05/trump -trade-master-plan-meets-car-conundrum/#5268065edbeb.

———. "Was Letting China into the WTO a Mistake?" *Foreign Affairs*, April 2, 2018. https://www.foreignaffairs.com/articles/china/2018 -04-02/was-letting-china-wto-mistake?cid=int-fls&pgtype=hpg.

———. "Will Trump's Tariffs Have a Silver Lining of Raising Revenue? Don't Bet on It." *Forbes*, April 12, 2018. https://www.forbes.com /sites/phillevy/2018/04/12/trump-tariff-revenue-what-tariff-revenue /#4d449346390f.

———. "With Brexit, President Trump Actually Gets It Right on Trade." *Forbes*, July 14, 2018. https://www.forbes.com/sites/phillevy/2018/07 /14/brexit-president-trump-gets-it-right-on-trade/#8adf663a9f01.

Levy, Phil, Javier Mancera, Daniel Schwanen, Jason Marczak, and Katherine Pereira. *What If NAFTA Ended?: The Imperative of a Successful Renegotiations*. Washington, DC: The Atlantic Council, 2017. http://www.atlanticcouncil.org/images/AC_NAFTA_100517_web.pdf.

Lynch, David, and Damian Paletta. "Trump Announces Steel and Aluminum Tariffs Thursday Over Objections from Advisers and Republicans." *The Washington Post*, March 1, 2018. https://www .washingtonpost.com/news/business/wp/2018/03/01/white-house -planning-major-announcement-thursday-on-steel-and-aluminum -imports/?noredirect=on&utm_term=.6ba72cc30b3e.

Mankiw, Greg. "The Current Account vs the Trade Deficit." *Random Observations for Students of Economics* (blog), July 1, 2006. https://gregmankiw.blogspot.com/2006/07/current-acccount-vs -trade-deficit.html.

Maverick, J. B. "What Is the Difference Between a Current Account Deficit and a Trade Deficit?" Investopedia, January 25, 2018. https://www.investopedia.com/ask/answers/010715/what-difference -between-current-account-deficit-and-trade-deficit.asp.

Monbiot, George. "Chlorinated Chicken? Yes, We Really Can Have Too Much Trade." *The Guardian*, July 25, 2017. https://www.theguardian .com/commentisfree/2017/jul/25/chlorinated-chicken-trade-britain -us-food-standards-globalisation.

Morrison, Wayne M. "China's Status as a Nonmarket Economy (NME)." News release IFI0385, Congressional Research Service, January 10, 2019. https://fas.org/sgp/crs/row/IF10385.pdf.

"NAFTA Debate: Gore vs. Perot." *Larry King Live*, CCN, November 9, 1993. http://ggallarotti.web.wesleyan.edu/govt155/goreperot.htm.

Office of the United States Trade Representative. "Bipartisan Trade Deal." May 2007. https://ustr.gov/sites/default/files/uploads /factsheets/2007/asset_upload_file127_11319.pdf.

———. "Labor Advisory Committee Members." https://ustr.gov/about-us /advisory-committees/labor-advisory-committee-lac.

———. "Peru Trade Promotion Agreement." https://ustr.gov/trade -agreements/free-trade-agreements/peru-tpa.

———. "The People's Republic of China." https://ustr.gov/countries -regions/china-mongolia-taiwan/peoples-republic-china.

Oppermann, Kai, and Klaus Brummer. "Veto Player Approaches in Foreign Policy Analysis." *Oxford Research Encyclopedias* (August 2017). http://doi.org/10.1093/acrefore/9780190228637.013.386.

Organisation for Economic Co-operation and Development. "Level of GDP Per Capita and Productivity." Data. Paris: OECD. https://stats .oecd.org/viewhtml.aspx?datasetcode=PDB_LV&lang=en.

Pelc, Krysztof. "The U.S. Broke a Huge Global Trade Taboo. Here's Why Trump's Move Might Be Legal." *The Washington Post*, June 7, 2018. https://www.washingtonpost.com/news/monkey-cage/wp/2018/06 /07/the-u-s-broke-a-huge-global-trade-taboo-heres-why-trumps -move-might-be-legal/?utm_term=.22472b8c4d33.

Picardo, Elvis. "Why China's Currency Tangos with the USD." Investope-dia, February 12, 2014. https://www.investopedia.com/articles /forex/09/chinas-peg-to-the-dollar.asp.

Pierce, Justin R., and Peter K. Schott. "The Surprisingly Swift Decline of US Manufacturing Employment." *American Economic Review* 106, no. 7 (July 2016): 1632–62. https://www.aeaweb.org/articles?id=10 .1257/aer.20131578.

Popper, Steven, Victoria Greenfield, Keith Crane, and Rehan Malik. *Measuring Economic Effects of Technical Barriers to Trade on U.S. Exporters.* Arlington, VA: RAND Science and Technology, 2004. https://www.nist.gov/sites/default/files/documents/director/planning /report04-3.pdf.

Prebisch, Raúl. "Theoretical and Practical Problems of Economic Growth." In *ECLAC Thinking, Selected Texts (1948-1998)*, edited by Ricardo Bielschowsky, 109–28. Santiago: ECLAC, 2016. https://repositorio.cepal.org/handle/11362/43904.

Putnam, Robert. "Diplomacy and Domestic Politics: The Logic of Two-Level Games." *International Organization* 42, no. 3 (1988): 427–60. http://www.jstor.org/stable/2706785.

Rasmussen, Chris. *Jobs Supported by Exports 2016: An Update*. Washington, DC: Office of Trade and Economic Analysis, Department of Commerce, International Trade Administration, August 2, 2017. https://www.trade.gov/mas/ian/build/groups/public/@tg_ian /documents/webcontent/tg_ian_005543.pdf.

Read, Robert. "The Political Economy of Trade Protection: The Determinants and Welfare Impact of the 2002 US Emergency Steel Safeguard Measures." *World Economy* 28, no. 8 (2005): 1119–37.

"Report of the Industry Trade Advisory Committee on Standards and Technical Barriers to Trade (ITAC 16)." Advisory Committee Report to the president, Congress and the United States Trade Representative on the Trans-Pacific Partnership Trade Agreement, December 2, 2015. https://ustr.gov/sites/default/files/ITAC-16-Standards-and -Technical-Barriers-to-Trade.pdf.

Reuters. "China Working-Age Population Shrinks, Presenting Pitfall for Pension Plans." Reuters, February 28, 2018. https://www.reuters.com /article/us-china-economy-population/china-working-age-population -shrinks-presenting-pitfall-for-pension-plans-idUSKCN1GC18C.

Rodriguez, Sabrina. "Pelosi Casts Doubt on Passage of Trump's New NAFTA Without Changes." *Politico*, December 6, 2018. https://www.politico.com/story/2018/12/06/pelosi-casts-doubt-on -trumps-usmca-passage-without-changes-1014361.

Rushford, Greg. "Trump's War on the WTO." *The Wall Street Journal*, July 4, 2018. https://www.wsj.com/articles/trumps-war-on-the-wto -1530723098.

"S. Korean Negotiator Vows to Put National Interest First in U.S. Trade Talks." Yonhap News Agency, January 5, 2018. http://english .yonhapnews.co.kr/business/2018/01/05/0502000000AEN 20180105000300315.html.

Sachs, Jeffrey D. "The Truth about Trade." *The Boston Globe*, October 17, 2016. https://www.bostonglobe.com/opinion/2016/10/16/the-truth- about-trade/UWtu8jpAo8LTsTFlffaZ0K/story.html.

Saikawa, Eri. "Policy Diffusion of Emission Standards Is There a Race to the Top?" *World Politics* 65, no. 1 (2013): 1–33. http://doi.org/10.1017 /S0043887112000238.

Schott, Jeffrey, and Euijin Jung. "KORUS Amendments: Minor Adjustments Fixed What Trump Called 'Horrible Trade Deal." Policy brief. Washington, DC: Peterson Institute for International Economics, November 2018. https://piie.com/system/files/documents/pb18-22.pdf.

Smeltz, Dina, Ivo Daalder, Karl Friedhoff, Craig Kafura, and Lily Wojtowicz. *America Engaged: American Public Opinion and US Foreign Policy*. Chicago: The Chicago Council on Global Affairs, 2018. https://digital.thechicagocouncil.org/america-engaged?_ga=2 .258877839.482070157.1547582270-1518113569.1485877455.

Smeltz, Dina, and Karen Whisler. *Pro-Trade Views on the Rise, Partisan Divisions on NAFTA Widen*. Chicago: The Chicago Council on Global Affairs, August 14, 2017. https://www.thechicagocouncil.org /publication/pro-trade-views-rise-partisan-divisions-nafta-widen.

Srinivasan, Thirukodikaval. *Developing Countries and the Multilateral Trading System: From GATT to the Uruguay Round and the Future*. Boulder, CO: Westview Press, 2000.

"Statistics on UK-EU Trade." Briefing paper, number 7851, House of Commons Library, January 11, 2019. https://researchbriefings.files .parliament.uk/documents/CBP-7851/CBP-7851.pdf.

Taylor, Adam. "A Timeline of Trump's Complicated Relationship with the TPP." *The Washington Post*, April 13, 2018. https://www .washingtonpost.com/news/worldviews/wp/2018/04/13/a -timeline-of-trumps-complicated-relationship-with-the-tpp/ ?utm_term=.521118af09d9.

"Trump Executive Order Pulls Out of TPP Trade Deal." BBC, January 24, 2017. https://www.bbc.com/news/world-us-canada-38721056.

"Trump Says He Made Up Facts About Trade Deficit in Meeting with Trudeau." CBC, March 15, 2018. https://www.cbc.ca/news/politics /trump-trudeau-1.4577179.

Tucker, Todd. "Are National Security Tariffs Legal?" *Medium*, February 16, 2018. https://medium.com/@toddntucker/are-national-security -tariffs-legal-2e8b0188a170.

United States Chamber of Commerce. *NAFTA Triumphant: Assessing Two Decades of Gains in Trade, Jobs, and Growth*. Washington, DC: U.S. Chamber of Commerce, October 2015. https://www .uschamber.com/report/nafta-triumphant-assessing-two-decades -gains-trade-growth-and-jobs.

United States Department of Commerce. "AutoAlliance232Comments _FINAL" Auto Alliance letter to Secretary Wilbur Ross, June 27, 2018. https://www.regulations.gov/document?D=DOC-2018-0002-1834.

———. "Section 323 Investigations: The Effects of Imports on the National Security." Washington, DC: Bureau of Industry and Security, US Department of Commerce. https://www.bis.doc.gov/232.

———. *The Compilation of World Motor Import Requirements*. Washington, DC: United States Department of Commerce, Office of Transportation and Machinery, 2011. https://www.trade.gov/d/otm/assets/auto/autos_tradebarriers2011.pdf.

———. *The Effect of Imports of Steel on the National Security*. Washington, DC: US Department of Commerce, January 11, 2018. https://www.bis.doc.gov/index.php/documents/steel/2224-the-effect-of-imports-of-steel-on-the-national-security-with-redactions-20180111/file.

———. "U.S. International Trade in Goods and Services November 2018." News release CB 19-05, BEA 19-02. Washington, DC: Bureau of Economic Analysis, US Department of Commerce, February 6, 2019. https://www.bea.gov/system/files/2019-02/trad1118_4.pdf.

United States Department of Defense. "Response to Steel and Aluminum Policy Recommendations." Memorandum from the Department of Defense to the Department of Commerce. https://www.commerce.gov/sites/default/files/department_of_defense_memo_response_to_steel_and_aluminum_policy_recommendations.pdf.

United States Department of Labor. *Report to the Committee on Finance of the Senate and the Committee on Ways and Means of the House of Representatives*. Washington, DC: The United States Department of Labor, Employment and Training Administration, 2015. https://www.doleta.gov/tradeact/docs/AnnualReport15.pdf.

———. "Trade Adjustment Assistance for Workers." https://www.doleta.gov/tradeact.

United States Department of Labor, Bureau of Labor Statistics. "Job Openings and Labor Turnover Survey." https://www.bls.gov/jlt.

United States Department of State. "Transatlantic Economic Council." https://www.state.gov/p/eur/rt/eu/tec.

———. "U.S. Collective Defense Arrangements." Last modified 2004. https://www.state.gov/s/l/treaty/collectivedefense.

United States Department of the Treasury. *Macroeconomic and Foreign Exchange Policies of Major Trading Partners of the United States*. Washington, DC: Office of International Affairs, US Department of the Treasury, October 2018. https://home.treasury.gov/system/files/206/2018-10-17-%28Fall-2018-FX%20Report%29.pdf.

United States Food and Drug Administration. "What Are 'Biologics' Questions and Answers." https://www.fda.gov/aboutfda/centersoffices/officeofmedicalproductsandtobacco/cber/ucm133077.htm.

United States International Trade Commission. "Understanding Anti-dumping & Countervailing Duty Investigations." https://www.usitc .gov/press_room/usad.htm.

———. "Understanding Safeguard Investigations." https://www.usitc.gov /press_room/us_safeguard.htm.

United States Trade Representative. *2017 Report to Congress on China's WTO Compliance*. Washington, DC: Office of the United States Trade Representative, January 2018. https://ustr.gov/sites/default /files/files/Press/Reports/China%202017%20WTO%20Report.pdf.

———. *Findings of the Investigation into China's Acts, Policies, and Practices Related to Technology Transfer, Intellectual Property, and Innovation Under Section 301 of the Trade Act of 1974*. Washington, DC: Office of the United States Trade Representative, March 22, 2018. https://ustr.gov/sites/default/files/Section%20301%20FINAL.PDF.

———. *Korea Memorandum of Understanding Regarding Foreign Motor Vehicles*. Washington, DC: United States Trade Representative, The Office of Trade Agreements Negotiation and Compliance, October 20, 1998. https://tcc.export.gov/Trade_Agreements/All_Trade _Agreements/exp_005688.asp.

———. "President Trump Approves Relief for U.S. Washing Machine and Solar Cell Manufacturers." Washington, DC: Office of the United States Trade Representative, January 22, 2018. https://ustr.gov /about-us/policy-offices/press-office/press-releases/2018/january /president-trump-approves-relief-us.

———. *Section 301 Enforcements and List, China 2018*. Washington, DC: Office of the United States Trade Representative. https://ustr.gov /sites/default/files/enforcement/301Investigations/List%201.pdf.

———. "Statement by Ambassador Robert E. Lighthizer on Retaliatory Duties." Press release. Washington, DC: Office of the United States Trade Representative, June 2018. https://ustr.gov/about-us/policy -offices/press-office/press-releases/2018/june/statement -ambassador-robert-e.

———. "The People's Republic of China." Washington, DC: Office of the United States Trade Representative. https://ustr.gov/countries -regions/china-mongolia-taiwan/peoples-republic-china.

U.S. Constitution. Article 1. Sec. 8. https://www.usconstitution.net/xconst _A1Sec8.html.

"US Sets Final Tariffs on Softwood Lumber from Canada." BBC, November 2, 2017. https://www.bbc.com/news/world-us-canada-41838828.

Villarreal, Angeles M., and Ian F. Fergusson. *The North American Free Trade Agreement (NAFTA)*. Washington, DC: Congressional Research Service, 2014.

Volcovici, Valerie. "Mary Landrieu Set to Take Over Senate Energy Panel Chair." *The Huffington Post*, February 11, 2014. https://www.huffington-post.com/2014/02/11/mary-landrieu-senate-energy_n_4770373.html.

von der Burchard, Hans, Megan Cassella, and Ginger Hervey. "A New Approach to EU-US Trade: Less Is More." *Politico*, September 17, 2018. https://www.politico.eu/article/donald-trump-eu-eye-trade-low -hanging-fruit.

Warren, Elizabeth. "The Trans-Pacific Partnership Clause Everyone Should Oppose." *The Washington Post*, February 25, 2015. https://www.washingtonpost.com/opinions/kill-the-dispute -settlement-language-in-the-trans-pacific-partnership/2015/02/25 /ec7705a2-bd1e-11e4-b274-e5209a3bc9a9_story.html?utm _term=.6e3576fb9ed2.

Weisman, Steven. "Bush and Democrats in Accord on Trade Deals." *The New York Times*, May 11, 2007. https://www.nytimes.com/2007/05 /11/business/11trade.html.

"What Donald Trump Means by Fair Trade." *The Economist*, May 13, 2017. https://www.economist.com/briefing/2017/05/13/what-donald -trump-means-by-fair-trade.

"What Is the Impossible Trinity?" *The Economist*, September 10, 2016. https://www.economist.com/the-economist-explains/2016/09/09 /what-is-the-impossible-trinity.

The White House. "Remarks by President Barack Obama at Suntory Hall." Office of the Press Secretary, The White House, November 14, 2009. https://obamawhitehouse.archives.gov/the-press-office /remarks-president-barack-obama-suntory-hall.

Wingrove, Josh, and Yako Takeo. "Gears of WTO Could Soon Halt Amid U.S. Concerns, Canada Warns." *Bloomberg*, January 20, 2019. https://www.bloomberg.com/news/articles/2019-01-20/gears-of-wto -could-soon-halt-amid-u-s-concerns-canada-warns.

The World Bank. "Current Account Balance (% of GDP)." Data on Germany and France. Geneva: The World Bank), https://data.worldbank. org/indicator/BN.CAB.XOKA.GD.ZS?end=2017&locations=DE-FR &start=1971&view=chart.

———. "GDP (Current US$)." Data on the world. Washington, DC: The World Bank. https://data.worldbank.org/indicator/NY.GDP.MKTP.CD ?end=2017&locations=US-1W&start=1960.

———. "GDP Per Capita (Current US$)." Data on China and the United States. Washington, DC: The World Bank, 2017. https://data .worldbank.org/indicator/NY.GDP.PCAP.CD?locations=CN-US.

———. "Services, Value Added (% of GDP)." Data on the United States. Washington, DC: The World Bank. https://data.worldbank.org /indicator/NV.SRV.TOTL.ZS?locations=US.

———. "Services, Value Added (% of GDP)." Data on the United States and the OECD members. Washington, DC: The World Bank. https://data .worldbank.org/indicator/NV.SRV.TOTL.ZS?locations=US-OE.

———. "Tariff Rate, Applied, Weighted Mean, All Products (%)." Data on the United States. Washington, DC: The World Bank. https://data .worldbank.org/indicator/TM.TAX.MRCH.WM.AR.ZS?locations=US.

World Intellectual Property Organization. https://www.wipo.int/portal /en/index.html.

World Trade Organization. "3 December — The Final Day and What Happens Next." Briefing note. https://www.wto.org/english /thewto_e/minist_e/min99_e/english/about_e/resum03_e.htm.

———. "Agreement on Subsidies and Countervailing Measures ('SCM Agreement')." https://www.wto.org/english/tratop_e/scm_e/subs _e.htm.

———. "Article XXI: Security Exceptions." In *General Agreement on Tariffs and Trade (GATT)*. Geneva: World Trade Organization. https://www.wto.org/english/res_e/booksp_e/gatt_ai_e/art21_e.pdf.

———. "Dispute Settlement." https://www.wto.org/english/tratop_e /dispu_e/dispu_e.htm.

———. "European Communities – Certain Measures Affecting Poultry Meat and Poultry Meat Products from the United States." https://www.wto.org/english/tratop_e/dispu_e/cases_e/ds389 _e.htm.

———. "Members and Observers." Data. Washington, DC: World Trade Organization. https://www.wto.org/english/res_e/statis_e/daily _update_e/tariff_profiles/E28_E.pdf.

———. "Export Competition/Subsidies." https://www.wto.org/english/tratop_e/agric_e/ag_intro04_export_e.htm.

———. "Information Technology Agreement." https://www.wto.org/english/tratop_e/inftec_e/inftec_e.htm.

———. "International Trade and Market Access Data." https://www.wto .org/english/res_e/statis_e/statis_bis_e.htm?solution=WTO&path =/Dashboards/MAPS&file=Map.wcdf&bookmarkState={%22impl%22 :%22client%22,%22params%22:{%22langParam%22:%22en%22}}.

———. "Members and Observers." https://www.wto.org/english /thewto_e/whatis_e/tif_e/org6_e.htm.

———. "Mexico and the WTO." https://www.wto.org/english/thewto_e
/countries_e/mexico_e.htm.

———. "Special and Differential Treatment Provisions." https://www.wto
.org/english/tratop_e/devel_e/dev_special_differential_provisions
_e.htm.

———. "Standards and Safety." https://www.wto.org/english/thewto_e
/whatis_e/tif_e/agrm4_e.htm.

———. "The GATT Years: From Havana to Marrakesh." https://www.wto
.org/english/thewto_e/Whatis_e/tif_e/fact4_e.htm.

———. *The Road to Doha and Beyond – A Road Map for Successfully
Concluding the Doha Development Agenda*. Geneva: World Trade
Organization, January 2002. https://www.wto.org/english/res_e
/booksp_e/roadtodoha_e.pdf.

———. "The WTO Agreement on the Application of Sanitary and Phytosanitary Measures (SPS Agreement)." https://www.wto.org/english
/tratop_e/sps_e/spsagr_e.htm.

———. "Trade-Related Aspects of Intellectual Property Rights."
https://www.wto.org/english/tratop_e/trips_e/trips_e.htm.

———. *United States – Certain Measures on Steel and Aluminum Products – Request for Consultations by Canada*. Geneva: World Trade
Organization, June 6, 2018. https://docs.wto.org/dol2fe/Pages/FE
_Search/FE_S_S006.aspx?Query=(%20@Symbol=%20(wt/ds550/1
%20))&Language=ENGLISH&Context=FomerScriptedSearch
&languageUIChanged=true.

———. "United States – Definitive Safeguard Measures of Imports of
Certain Steel Products." https://www.wto.org/english/tratop_e
/dispu_e/cases_e/ds252_e.htm.

———. "United States – Measures Affecting Imports of Poultry Products."
https://www.wto.org/english/tratop_e/dispu_e/cases_e/ds100_e.htm.

———. "United States of America." http://stat.wto.org/CountryProfile
/WSDBCountryPFView.aspx?Language=E&Country=US.

———. "United States and European Auto Tariff Schedule." Data. Washington, DC: World Trade Organization. http://tariffdata.wto.org
/ReportersAndProducts.aspx.

———. "United States of America." Data. Washington, DC: World Trade
Organization. https://www.wto.org/english/res_e/statis_e/daily
_update_e/tariff_profiles/US_E.PDF.

Zhu, Xiaodong. "Understanding China's Growth: Past, Present, and
Future." *Journal of Economic Perspectives* 26, no. 4 (2012): 103–24.
http://doi.org/10.1257/jep.26.4.103.